THE ARTS ON CAMPUS:

THE NECESSITY FOR CHANGE

BY

JAMES ACKERMAN

PETER CAWS

ERIC LARRABEE

NORMAN LLOYD

MARGARET MAHONEY

JON ROUSH

ROBERT WATTS

KENNETH WINTER

EDITED BY

MARGARET MAHONEY

WITH THE ASSISTANCE OF

ISABEL MOORE

The Arts on Campus:

THE NECESSITY FOR CHANGE

NEW YORK GRAPHIC SOCIETY LTD.

Greenwich, Connecticut

International Standard Book No. 0-8212-0392-4
Library of Congress Catalog Card No. 72-110664

Printed and bound
in the United States of America

CONTENTS

III

APPENDIX

FOREWORD

The need for change in teaching the arts to undergraduates was from the beginning the common concern of the authors and became the theme of the book. We started off with the hope that the book would be a joint venture in which the authors could pool their ideas about how teaching in the arts should be altered. This aim was achieved.

We have used the word "arts" in various ways: to cover fields, in some instances, or to mean special things, in others. One author may use it when discussing the content of culture, another when writing about the visual arts, still another when referring only to studio programs and someone else when expostulating about historical study. Thus the word has different meaning for different people and the reader will have to read the book with this in mind, understanding how difficult it is to carefully define a term that can cover so much and mean so many things.

Part I introduces the theme of the need for change. The opening chapter entitled "The Theme: A Sense of Loss," is a personal comment by a student and was a letter in its original form. It has been selected to open the book because it presents a reaction that many colleges have failed to legitimatize, but one that I have heard expressed often. It reveals the depth of a student's frustration in trying to organize his formal education; and it suggests by its title, and between the lines, a failure on the part of at least one institution to recognize the potential importance of the arts in college education. The author is Kenneth Winter, who is now in a graduate program in psychology at the University of Michigan, Ann Arbor.

In the pages that follow, I trace the development of my own involvement with the problems in teaching the arts in the colleges, how this led to the book, and what the authors hoped to accomplish in writing the book. My interest in how the arts are taught developed out of training which I had in the visual arts, and out of two work experiences: my present position as an officer at Carnegie Corporation of New York, a foundation which has always been involved in programs to improve

American education at all levels; and my earlier work with the UNESCO Relations Staff in the U.S. Department of State, an assignment which was concerned with putting American artists and teachers of the arts in touch with their counterparts in other countries.

Part II is the heart of the book. The authors in this section are concerned about current practices in teaching the arts. All believe that a restructuring of educational goals and course work is overdue. The assumption throughout is that the setting for teaching has to become freer and more open to new ideas than it now can be, if experiments in the educational process are to take place. Each chapter is preceded by an introduction which I have written to provide continuity for the book, and pertinent biographical information about the contributors.

Part III is a summation of our concerns as authors. It is a rounding out of our opinion, and a drawing together of what we think are the most important recommendations for change. It was written by Jon Roush on behalf of the group.

Although I have acted as general editor of the book, all along the way I have had the interest and help of all of the authors. We have shared ideas through meetings, by letters, and in talks, and the result has been a collaboration which has resulted in a genuine group project.

Several other people helped to bring the book into being, each contributing something special and personal: Florence Anderson, Beulah Bumford, Lorenz Eitner, Barbara Finberg, Caroline Hightower, Allan Kaprow, Odessa McClain, Nell Mahoney, Barbara Newsom, Robert Oksner, Alan Pifer, and Helen Rowan. For the survey of college arts programs which I refer to and summarize in the book, I had access to good advice from Lloyd Morrissett, Brant Sloan, and Margo Viscusi and some unusual talent at Carnegie Corporation, which included Brenda Jubin, Mary Pugh Clark, Martha Kowal Crawford, and Lonnie Sharpe.

The publisher of the book is a company I admire and my experience in working with both Burton Cumming and Forrest Selvig at New York Graphic proves to me the value of interested editors.

MARGARET MAHONEY

8

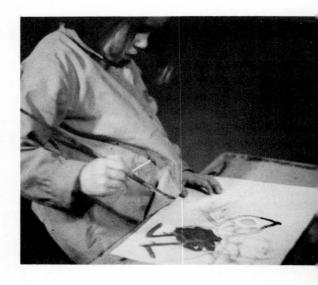

". . . to counterbalance
cultural blocks to
perception and visual
communication and to
restore the natural
capacities for making
and understanding images
that children in our
culture display in
pre-adolescent years."

from James Ackerman,
"Education of Vision."

". . . the exercise of art
in action—the actual
practice of communication
between the student in
art and an audience."

from James Ackerman,
"Education of Vision."

"There is a breaking down of arbitrary differences that have been built up between so-called 'high' and 'low,' 'native' and 'exotic' cultures."

from Norman Lloyd, "Music and Education."

". . . we have the means and the will to give utopia a try."

from Jon Roush, "Epilogue."

"The kind of art that can control the way we project ourselves in the world will perhaps be most like the art of a happening, in which an event and an environment mutually inform each other, in which each individual is a creative participant within a surrounding form."

from Jon Roush,
"The Humanities Museum."

"They deny economic man; they announce Daniel Bell's post-industrial man, and not a few of them have arrived at Bell's end of ideology."

from Eric Larrabee,
"Artist and University."

I

The Theme: A Sense of Loss

KENNETH WINTER

When I entered the university's art program as a freshman, my reasons for being there seemed clear to me. I had "talent": a knack for making photograph-like drawings and nicely balanced compositions. I believed, thanks to reading advertisements for art schools, that one could make a secure living with such skills. I liked being praised for my drawings and cartoons, and was vaguely aware of an intrinsic satisfaction that did not depend on hearing applause. And after twelve years of schooling, I was vividly aware of a desire to stay as far away from term papers and libraries as possible.

My outlook was characteristic of many new art students. It was not, I think, hopeless. The intrinsic joy of creation was already, confusedly, within me. And I was ready—as I discovered later—to put energy into activities that promised to make society more livable.

But, as a college freshman, I was not yet able to take the intrinsic satisfaction of art-working seriously. I came from a literal, utilitarian, no-nonsense kind of background: any serious activity (the stuff of which respectable careers are made) had to be good for something. If you enjoyed the doing itself, you had better make extra sure you were doing something productive, to justify such self-indulgence. I needed to become aware of the satisfaction of doing and to accept the pleasure of creating as an important indication of the likely value of the creation.

More important was my total lack of experience in simply trying to live in the world at large. Surrounded by suburban high-school society and television culture, I had not been exactly immersed in life. I had never made a consequential decision, taken an irreversible risk, had (or tried and failed to have) an effect on my society, nor assumed responsibility for someone else. I had no idea that there were possibilities and problems in the world, to which artistic creation could come as a response and a solution.

In this vacuum of experience, I could not see art as being good for anything. I could hardly be expected to experience art (or for that matter, any advanced subject) as anything but a technical exercise, useful only for giving urban intellectuals something to talk about.

This was my starting point. If I was ever to be an artist, this was where my art education would have to begin. Unfortunately, I was largely unaware of my needs, so I could not effectively insist that they be met. And to the extent that I was aware, I was kept docile by a faith that the faculty knew what they were doing, that they certainly would make sure I got whatever one needs to be an artist—not merely the techniques of art, but the key to satisfaction and purpose as well. For my part, I had only to be a good student and everything would fall into place.

In fact, all that the faculty offered was technical instruction, and even that was lackadaisical. My three semesters in art school consisted of a series of assigned projects, each with a deadline a week or so away and followed immediately by another assignment. Each one graded, of course. In between the deadlines, the teacher would wander into the room occasionally and make comments on our work—comments such as "Hmmm. Interesting." Most of my effort during those wasted sixteen months was spent meeting the deadlines.

My growing worries about purpose and satisfaction remained underground. The other students either seemed not to care what art was doing for them and for the world, or else seemed already to know, in some way that was beyond my comprehension. The faculty did nothing to prompt us to work on such basic questions. When confronted with a "What good is all this?" question, they seemed as lost as the students. In the mood of the art school, there was no sense that here was a place where people were engaged in doing necessary and significant things, where one could feel enthusiasm and commitment just by being there. All in all, it felt like one of society's backwaters, hardly the place for one not yet resigned. In such surroundings, I never thought about the possibility of sharing my concerns regarding what art was all about, let alone actively working with others on them as an integral part of our education.

Instead I brooded about them by myself. This strategy, of course, closed me off from learning anything. It left me a prisoner of my own literal mind and narrow experience. For example, I heard that a man did an art work because he had "something to express." That struck me as being perverse of him. If he had something so damned important to tell us, why obscure the message by putting it in a painting (or novel, etc.)? Why didn't he just *tell* us? I heard people talk about "art for its own sake," which in my experience made no sense at all. All I could guess was that they understood something that I wasn't even aware of. Okay, I decided, if I just think hard and carefully and logically enough, I can figure out what this Pure Art is. Then I can do it precisely, exactly right, paint the perfect painting, after which all painters will close up shop. This ultimate painting would be one which, when you looked at it, would give you such a thrill that you would stand there transfixed forever, in a sort of lifelong orgasm.

Predictably, these private fantasies remained private and remained fantasies. Meanwhile, my first contacts with the infant "new left" (this was 1961) showed me that there *were* problems in society and that there *were* things to do about them. Neither my private fantasies nor the artist's world I was seeing in art school showed any relation to these problems. "Serious" art seemed to be, in the end, nothing but an esoteric branch of the entertainment industry. The function of commercial art was more apparent, but I had better things to do than "help somebody peddle underwear," as I recall putting it at the time. I felt my non-art-school friends were learning all sorts of important and powerful things, while I sat doing play-school projects.

So I got out. I have never regretted it. And I've never since touched a paintbrush or a bottle of India ink, or even taken any courses in "the humanities" at all.

Overview
of the
Present

MARGARET MAHONEY

In my work I meet and listen to many people. It is one of the means that a foundation has for learning what individuals are thinking about, their views, and their concerns. Most of the talk is about particular projects and possibilities of funding, but there are times when it is less precise, and financing—at least at that moment—is not an issue. It is this kind of informal exchange that encourages frank opinion and sometimes leads to the definition of a problem before it is generally clear that a problem exists. This happened for me in the arts.

About five years ago, after a succession of talks with students, professors, and administrators, I started to question in my own mind the relationship between the universities and the arts. In most of the discussions we had been airing ideas; we rarely talked about foundation money, since Carnegie was not making grants to either artists or college art projects. But my own personal interest in the arts and the foundation's interest in keeping informed meant not only that our door was open but that I made a point when on a campus to see a variety of individuals, many of whom had an interest in the arts. The talks I had led me to speculate that, while it seemed to make sense for the universities to provide students with the opportunity to learn about the arts, the way in which the arts happened to be taught at a university might not be how students in fact learn them.

Students gave me the first indication of the ill-fit between the arts and the rest of the college. Kenneth Winter's experiences in art school, which he recounts in the opening chapter, "The Theme: A Sense of Loss," were similar to those reported by many of the students I met. They confessed that it was hard for them to see any value in studying art. What they wanted was to understand themselves and their community, and they found the social sciences more appealing. Those who wanted to study art, because they had either talent or some intellectual curiosity, complained of such inflexibilities as a tight academic calendar which meant that art could not be fitted in, or assigned hours when studio space was available.

These comments were not confined to any one art but applied to music, theater, and the visual arts, and to studio work as well as history and appreciation courses. I began to sense, therefore, the enormity of the problem, particularly when I considered the possibility that these kinds of concerns might be general throughout the nation.

The deans who talked to me about their concerns expressed frustration with faculty who could not give any understandable rationale for including the arts in the undergraduate curriculum, a statement that the deans felt they needed if they were to support faculty requests for additional funds and for more courses.

Some department heads confessed similar frustration in trying to get faculty members to meet their practical demands for justifying the arts in a college program. But there were others who agreed with individual faculty members that the simple point is that art is an integral part of society and that as such it has an important place on a college campus.

Generally, however, neither teachers nor administrators believed that the problem was so simple. They raised such serious questions as whether any professional training can be done at a university or college, whether the detachment that characterizes most universities in relation to the outside world means that the arts cannot flourish on campus, whether any attempt to reach the mass of students is too little and too late since most students come to college with preconceived notions about the arts or no notions and no interest.

At this particular point in my own thinking I was asked to do a survey for the Carnegie Foundation for the Advancement of Teaching. It was to be a quick review for some of the foundation's trustees who were college presidents and wanted to scrutinize their arts offerings. My survey, completed in the fall of 1967, included the visual arts, music, theater, and film and was based on an analysis of college catalogs, campus visits, correspondence, talks with individuals teaching or directing programs at the college level, and any available writing about the status of university programs in the arts. One of the most valuable reports was *The Visual Arts in Higher Education,* a study of 264 institutions published by the College Art Association. This, combined with my review, which covered 35 colleges, seemed to give a fairly accurate picture of college programs in the visual arts. Nothing comparable was available in other art fields, except for useful statistics compiled by the American Educational Theatre Association and for one report on film programs prepared by the American Council on Education.

The present book grew out of my limited survey, which I sent to several people for comments. Thoughtful letters came in reply, and these reinforced my feeling that there was an uneasy relationship between the arts and the universities, perhaps even an unnatural one. I thought that the problem was immense, however, and would not have confronted it except for a challenge from Burton Cumming, Editor-in-Chief at New York Graphic Society Ltd. Cumming felt that if the situation on campuses was as bad as my review indicated, then I, or someone, ought to report it to a wider audience. He added that his own experience made him think that the situation was serious and he offered to publish what might result from another look at the problem. Intrigued with the challenge, I began to talk with a few individuals whom I knew would agree that there were distinctive problems for colleges which wanted to include the arts in higher education. Each of them saw and discussed the problems differently but each started from a common base of concern, and I decided that if a book were to be written it should be a group project and that these were the people to include. Each agreed to write at least one chapter and to do so from his particular point of view. I felt that the differences in views among the authors, which stemmed from differences in training and experience, were important if we were to sort out the real and soluble problems.

Our point of departure was my 1967 College Survey in which I had identified some of the problems, most of which I felt reflected weaknesses in university planning. The first of these is the absolute separation of the arts, with very little evidence of interdepartmental cooperation or recognition of common interests. Since artists in any field have some conscious or instinctive awareness of the other arts, the university's segmented way of presenting the arts to students seemed to contradict what goes on in the real world of the arts. Separatism in college teaching therefore could be a serious weakness, reducing the effectiveness of teaching, giving students only one way of seeing or studying a problem. In any case, separatism inhibits interdepartmental cooperation since it reinforces the defenses of professors who prefer to see their art within its special set of circumstances. The summary of my 1967 survey is in the back of the book as part of the Appendix. It shows how the teaching has been organized for departmental and interdepartmental offerings.

The second problem is student interests and values. Art departments may talk about reaching out to more students and express pride in increased enrollment, but they have been quick to point out that handling more students means more time, more space, and more faculty. In most discussions of this problem there has been little recognition that new ways may have to be found to reach large numbers of students, and that student differences, not only in aptitude but in degree of interest, are relevant in planning an arts curriculum.

The annual survey by the American Council on Education (ACE) of incoming freshmen at 358 colleges has shown for the last two years that roughly 8 per cent are thinking about a major in one of the arts. The other students probably fall into one of the following categories: indifferent toward the arts; busy in other areas; fundamentally suspicious of the arts; too conscious of inaptitude to enroll in courses with more talented students. I cannot substantiate this conjecture, but students themselves confirm that, in general, half the student population is totally uninterested in the arts. I suspect that the attitudes range from the view that the arts are non-utilitarian to the one that they are non-intellectual activity reserved for women and non-masculine males. We know from several studies, including the ACE survey of freshmen, that the majority of students go to college to acquire a marketable skill and to make friends, and that few students see the arts as directly relevant to those objectives. But over two-thirds of the freshmen have stated that one of their reasons for going to college is also to seek a philosophy of life. The fact that relatively few students, in proportion to those who as freshmen have stated such a goal, enroll in arts courses during four years at college, suggests that few students think of the arts as relevant to their search for a philosophy of life.

A third problem that can be identified as a weakness in university planning vis-à-vis the arts is the lack of relationship or coordination between the regular curriculum and the extracurricular. In my college survey there were only two explicit examples of efforts to tie together the two, both in music. At Indiana University and Kalamazoo College classroom instruction was related to music being performed during the year on campus or in the area. I found no recorded evidence that any of the 35 colleges looked to student-generated extracurricular activity for ideas that might be used in the classroom, yet I know from students and teachers that there are many undocumented instances in which student-sponsored activity has in fact stimulated recent course work in film and photography, and did so years ago in theater and in music. (Courses openly initiated by students would thus have been a phenomenon two years ago, but as of 1969 some colleges are not only allowing it but encouraging it.)

The fourth problem is the lack of correlation between curriculum planning and physical design of facilities for the arts. Raising funds for arts buildings seems to be relatively easy as compared to finding money for course work, whether a small independent college is involved or a large university. There are donors who are expressly and only interested in the arts, and in building a building. There are none that I am aware of who have provided funds for a thorough curriculum review before an architect is called in. Apart from the Hopkins Center at Dartmouth and

Stanford University's new visual arts center I did not find any new facility in the arts that was preceded by serious curricular review and planning which then in turn was allowed to affect the design of a building.

As in the case of the Yale school of art and architecture, a building program can dictate what is learned. At Yale, the interior of the school is so constructed that space circumscribes activity, and students resort to temporary walls to provide some semblance of individual studio space. The impression made on the visitor is that no thought was given to the possibility that new kinds of art forms may demand new kinds of space and technology, and that the architects of such buildings have allowed their interest in creating a satisfying outward image to override any interest in providing space that will adapt to function. The ultimate responsibility lies with the universities, which are caught up in the effort to raise money for new buildings and in the process have neglected the question of curriculum review. First priority should go to a reconsideration of program, but in fairness to the faculty and the administration I admit that limited financial resources for such review or planning probably restrict thinking on the issue.

Nonetheless, my conclusion after finishing the survey in 1967 was that means have to be found for effecting change in teaching the arts, and a proposal for a new building is one means of initiating a review of current practices at a college or of possible programs for a new college. And ideally, such a review should also cover the feasibility of adapting old structures or using new kinds of industrial design for certain artistic needs—open space, workshop areas, walls and floors that can take hard use.

Equally important, planning for college museums and art centers should start with the assumption that what goes on in these facilities is part of the total educational program of a college. Effort should be made to accommodate large groups and to encourage variety in what can be shown. Buildings should not go up without full consideration of the demands of art, particularly of new forms of art. Too often arts facilities are copies of metropolitan centers of art, with the emphasis on standard technology and with heavy investment of dollars that might be reduced or better used for larger, less luxurious, more flexible space.

Finally, as the result of my review, I have concluded that one major fault in college programs is the failure to acknowledge that what goes on in elementary and secondary education is relevant to college teaching.

The fault goes deeper because of the failure of colleges to take any responsibility, and thus any real interest, in what the schools do or do not offer.

These problems continued to involve me after my survey was completed, and as I confessed to Burton Cumming, I was bewildered by the complexity of seemingly simple issues. On the surface they were easily soluble. It was a matter of someone taking the initiative and making decisions on programmatic objectives and organizational patterns. But, setting objectives for a program depends on complete understanding of the relevant subjects, and a closer look at the teaching and study of the arts revealed that such understanding was missing. The arts were not only misunderstood in terms of their educational importance but in terms of their inherent importance—reason enough for producing a book.

This is a book therefore about change, in organization, in content, and in attitudes. It is written for all individuals who have a vested interest in the arts and this includes most students, many faculty, all deans, every president, and hopefully some trustees of colleges and universities. If we as authors have a bias it is that we believe that the nation's most explicit need is for citizens who will be creative participants in shaping environment and that the colleges have an unmet responsibility to provide an educational experience that will encourage students to accept this role. The arts become central in such an educational task and cannot be treated as extras or as the special province of artistically talented students. Nor can the artist-teachers be set aside for mere display purposes or given second-class status on a campus. The chapters that follow concern the need for changing attitudes and contain specific ideas for developing a setting in which the arts can be studied and in which artists as teachers and guides can be active participants in the educational process.

The book concerns all the arts, although there is not a chapter for each art field. The apparent emphasis on the visual arts and on music reflects the training of the authors, not prejudice, and in our study of the problem we have come to believe that one can generalize about the arts, that an example from one specific field can be applied—however loosely—to another field.

II

THREE

The Humanities Museum

JON ROUSH

The reasons that the arts have never been accepted as an integral part of undergraduate education are outlined by Jon Roush in this chapter, "The Humanities Museum." He is concerned with the concept of the museum as a storehouse of knowledge, a passive concept that he believes pervades humanities programs at most colleges. Our reverence for the past, and an emphasis on knowledge for its own sake, are the chief characteristics he ascribes to these programs. His suggestion is not that colleges should deemphasize scholarship but that they should develop a mode of rigorous scholarship in human affairs which is concerned with questions of values. In such a context, he would give first importance to the arts.

Jon Roush is assistant professor of literature and humanities at Reed College, Portland, Oregon. He was on leave 1967-69 to be at Carnegie Corporation. Before going to Reed he served as project secretary with the Educational Policies Commission. He has published poetry in little magazines and has contributed the article, "What Will Become of the Past," *to the summer 1969 issue of* Daedalus. *His book* The Shape of the Harp: Poems and Translations *was published by Amherst College Press in 1961.*

"Would you tell me, please, which way I ought to go from here?"

"That depends a good deal on where you want to get to," said the Cat.

"I don't much care where—" said Alice.

"Then it doesn't matter which way you go," said the Cat.

"—so long as I get *somewhere,*" Alice added as an explanation.

"Oh, you're sure to do that," said the Cat, "if you only walk long enough."

Alice's Adventures in Wonderland by Lewis Carroll

"Well here goes nothing."

Prisoner entering death chamber at San Quentin.

If anyone is looking for an epigraph for this age, I offer the two above. Alice's confusion is childlike, the confusion of pure hope, a subject looking for an object. The prisoner's despair is pure death, nothing entering nothingness. They are different responses to the same situation; Alice and the prisoner both find themselves enveloped by some mystifying process which seems to have nothing to do with their own wills. In such a situation, if you regard the process as relatively benign, you ask directions; if you regard it as less hopeful, you become resigned to a more apocalyptic view. To many people, one or the other of these responses seems appropriate to this period in history—a period, they feel, in which a man can no longer make choices for himself. The question is two-pronged: Where are we going, and could we do anything about it if we knew? Does our rationalized, technological society take matters into its machine-like hands so efficiently that all important decisions affecting our lives are inevitably made elsewhere?

If there is an answer, it involves education and art. Although it would be presumptuous to say that artists can solve the problems of the world, that presumption is less to be feared than the possibility that artists will turn their backs on the world. In education that kind of behavior would perpetuate some unfortunate distinctions between art and thought, and practical affairs. Such distinctions helped get us in trouble in the first place, and they are more than ever inappropriate. Our problem is not simply to encourage artists to be *engagés* but to give men the control over their lives and surroundings that artists have over their materials. That power is within our grasp for the first time in history, but to assume it wisely we will need to strike new alliances between the arts and the humanistic fields of scholarship—philosophy, history, and the academic study of literature and the arts. Living must become quite literally a more artistic enterprise, and that will require developing a new science of man which draws on and develops its own peculiar art forms.

In colleges and universities today, the humanities generally include those disciplines which study human creations and actions. Although it is difficult to say precisely what the disciplines in this grab bag have in common, in college curricula they are usually approached as the means to the study of a tradition. Almost invariably, that tradition matches exactly the development of Western civilization. It is a tradition which is assumed to be continuous down to modern times, and there is assumed agreement about which objects and events are most valuable and exemplary in that tradition. Many different objectives have been advanced for education in the humanities, but they generally fall within two broad objectives: either the development in students of some particularly humane way of looking at the world, or the transmission to students of key elements of the culture which they have inherited. In fact, however, the first objective has little effect on the shaping of humanities curricula, for the reason that few of us have had very clear ideas about how to develop in others a humane way of looking at things. As for the second, most of us hold pretty firm ideas about which are the key elements of our cultural heritage meriting preservation, and so by design or default the typical curriculum in the humanities is aimed at presenting those objects with which "any educated man" should be familiar. The typical humanities course or curriculum is a guided tour through a museum.

This approach makes the role of the arts problematic. The so-called creative arts are normally kept at arm's length from the humanities curriculum. Often they are not officially included among those disciplines listed as "humanities" in the catalogs, and when they are, it is usually in those courses which teach students to study the arts but not to practice them. Both the scholar and the artist suffer from the distinction, but more importantly, students suffer if they accept the implication that the distinction between art and serious thought is absolute. The distinction is *not* absolute, and if we take seriously the problem of preparing a student for the future, then we must take seriously the responsibility to help him become artful as well as knowledgeable.

At one time the museum approach might have been culturally satisfactory, although it has always been questionable pedagogy, but the traditional cultural foundation upon which it once rested is now being undermined from several directions. Its primary assumption is that objects and values will endure and therefore can be preserved, but even that assumption is being questioned with increasing cogency. Impermanence is a hallmark of this era, and although sensitive men in all times have been oppressed or exhilarated by the feeling that theirs was an age of unprecedented change, there is a new quality to the mutability of our age. It is not only swifter and more pervasive, but for the first time the whole society is explicitly organized to promote it. Each of us contributes to it. Each of us is working to produce next year's model, the newest wonder drug, the latest industrial complex which will require the next skyscraper which will produce the next alteration in the cityscape, the next cumulative addition to scholarship which will change our view of the past, the next fashionable artistic style.

In the context of organized impermanence, two questions arise concerning the museum concept.

The first is fairly obvious, although the answer is obscure: In a world committed to change, what kind of sense does it make to talk about enduring values? The works and events which are normally studied in the humanities are considered important both because they are deemed to represent the utmost men can perform and because they are part of a valued tradition. They endure because of their merit, and conversely, their durability proves their merit. Pindar was probably not the first poet to claim that his songs made him immortal, and Shakespeare was not the last. Yet although few people would predict the imminent eclipse of Shakespeare, the value of endurance no longer seems as great as it once did. Nor is our sense of tradition as sure as it once was, and consequently the justification of humanistic study as the preserver of pertinent traditions is increasingly questionable.

Some contemporary artists, experimenting with short-lived works and with techniques of mass production, have explicitly abjured the permanence of the unique work as a value. In doing so they have raised the second question posed by the museum concept: In a world committed to change, will it not be increasingly easy to objectify our most transient moods, and will our perception of the world itself not alter so that it will become increasingly difficult to see anything but a reflection of ourselves? The situation has been described most clearly by Kenneth Craik in a paper entitled "The Prospects for an Environmental Psychology."

The degree to which the shape of the physical environment will be made responsive to human intentions, and the speed of that responsiveness, will be vastly increased by developments in the technological means of altering the physical environment. One psychological result will be a diminishing of the distinction between matter and fantasy. Psychologically, an object appears to be a material entity if it is somewhat immutable and only slowly and effortfully responsive to human intentions, while an object seems fanciful if it is effervescent and quickly, effortlessly responsive to human intentions. Thus, one prediction I will hazard is that the physical environment will become less "material" and more whimsical, if not more "spiritual."

It would be interesting to see an elaboration of that idea by someone with psychiatric training, but even to the untrained observer it is instructive to look at our present environment as a set of objectified fantasies. Whatever their significance may be, the content of those fantasies is rather discouraging. Our environment seems to have been shaped by two controlling fantasies: one involving unlimited self-aggrandizement through spatial extension and the other involving death by strangulation or smothering. Both fantasies can evoke the same content: millions of miles of highways in the process of apparently infinite expansion; aircraft whose speed and capacity will apparently be increased indefinitely; nuclear delivery systems and lines of defense being placed and replaced, duplicated and reduplicated; cities growing and growing and growing; and the whole process consuming oxygen, fuel and other resources and leaving in their place a dismal array of pollutants. Our fantasies are compulsive: overpopulation, overcrowding, overkill. If, then, technology offers the means for making the world even more fantasy-like, we could be pardoned for declining to go along. Unfortunately, that seems to be one choice which realistically is not open to us, so we might more profitably spend our time improving the fantasies.

The missing factor in the nightmare being played around us is art. It is art which takes the content of fantasy and shapes it, controls it, limits it, and creates from it something humane. The problem facing us is not simply to learn to be more creative; one could argue that we are too zealously creative now. Even as we are creating a superabundance of people and things, we find it easier to continue to create more and more of both than to work to adapt that which exists. It requires a great deal of creativity to solve the problems involved in placing an airport in the middle of the Everglades, to obliterate a natural environment and replace it with an unstable, artificial one, but there are good reasons for regarding that creativity as misplaced.

Even the discipline of art, however, would not be sufficient to make a totally unresponsive environment bearable. It is here that the arts and the humanities must create a united front. We need to develop a mode of rigorous scholarship in human affairs which is imbued with artistic judgment of proportion, which is concerned with questions of values, and which has as its arena not just the museum but the marketplace or legislative chamber. The kind of art that can control the way we project ourselves in the world will perhaps be most like the art of a happening, in which an event and an environment mutually inform each other, in which each individual is a creative participant within a surrounding form. We are already beginning to take seriously the need for beauty in our environment. We must also begin to recognize the need for beauty in our processes and events. The humanistic disciplines are concerned with evaluating different kinds of human expression, and they should be able to deal with this kind as well. When is a political campaign or a meeting or the constructing of a building beautiful? How can they be structured so as to be beautiful? Such art would need to draw on the skills of the humanistic disciplines to approach fundamental questions of human values and to judge the expression of those values. It was, after all, Plato who first asked about the beauty of actions.

The two effects of impermanence—the apparent irrelevance of the past, and the eventful environment—both point to the need for a new kind of humanistic education which has as its objective that the expression of individual concerns shall be disciplined and shaped by art. We need to educate artist-artisans: men who are technologically skillful but whose sense of utility is tempered by the sensibility of art. They would have the power over themselves to reshape fantasy into objects and environments which would be most useful to most men. Some of them would be at home in corporate executive offices, some on zoning commissions, some in federal and state regulatory agencies. But, in fact, most people as voters and consumers need to be exposed to the artist-artisan's way of approaching a problem. Since technology has made our total environment our medium for expressing ourselves, we had better become accomplished in the art of using that medium.

The beginning and end of that art is self-knowledge. We are all living in an age in which one man's lifetime will bring problems which he cannot possibly foresee and for which there are no conventional solutions. He will still study works of the past, but their history will not be his. He will participate in traditions not as a discoverer but as an artist, whose one final truth is his own, for which he is accountable to the past but in his own way. Through his own choices he will be the creator of environments and events, and his entire lifetime will be a single tradition, perhaps the longest continuous tradition in which he will participate.

Man is becoming the most durable element in his material environment, and one man's memory is becoming the most durable element in his intellectual environment; consequently, in any discussion of humanistic education it is clear that we need to rethink the role of tradition. It is probably not appropriate to expect a university to reconstruct traditions. That has never been a university's task, and for good reasons. A tradition is different from history in that a tradition is kept alive by individuals who are responding to the demand of the past at the same time that they are responding to immediate and personal demands of their own. Consequently there is always a dialectical tension between the past and present instances of a tradition. If there is no such tension, we are dealing either with a cliché or with an invention. Because a tradition has no substance outside the recurrent expressions of men who participate in it, it requires continual re-creation as well as study. The role of education, then, is to make the past accessible to the student at the same time that it allows him to explore his own capacity for thought and action. In the arts as in all the humanities, colleges should prepare students for the revitalization of traditions in their own lives.

Few colleges have achieved such a role today. Usually, making the past accessible involves telling a student what to think about the past. Rarely is he encouraged to be challenged by the past, and if he does perceive such a challenge on his own, he soon learns not to confess it. Yet this kind of challenge is what traditions are all about. We must find ways for students to be challenged by the past and to challenge it, and it is here that the arts can be most useful. The museum concept of the humanities has never actually worked because men have always sought to reconstruct their own past, and the museum concept is particularly inappropriate now when the past often does not seem so much a burden as simply an irrelevancy. If the past can become relevant to a man who lives through the next fifty years, it will happen because he has been able to fashion his own statement of meaning and to test it against others, not because he feels heir to one past or another. He will not be interested in received opinions. For him the arts can provide the means for meaningful personal statements; and because products of the arts are, in a very real sense, timeless, the arts can provide a pattern for the present's challenge to the past.

The distinction made between a studio course and an academic course, or between literary criticism and creative writing, allows a student to "express himself" without having to answer to the past in any way. I have heard several teachers complain that students have a romantic notion of self-expression which ignores the necessity for hard work and discipline. Yet it is ironic that those same professors in their own courses rarely suggest ways for students to use their discipline for responsible self-expression. The sad outcome is that by enforcing the distinction between thinking and doing, professors of the humanities have permitted doing without thinking and thinking without doing. A course is merely academic if it fails to encourage students to make meaningful choices, choices that have real consequences for the student himself. Because such choices are difficult and because some people prefer to let others make choices for them, teachers in the arts must consciously strive to see that they are made. If a student in a course in music composition is asked to compose like Mozart, he may complete the exercise satisfactorily without making any judgments about his own commitments. He may learn about Mozart, and that is good; he may broaden his own repertoire of compositional styles, and that is better; but unless he is moved to take Mozart personally, as a friend or a foe, he will not be able to make his own way in the musical environment which Mozart helped create. He may remember enough Mozart to pass an examination, but unless it is the kind of personal memory which brings order to the present and suggests the future, his memory will be useless. He might as well have amnesia. Our society is peopled by artistic amnesiacs. Men come out of humanities courses in some of the "best" colleges in the country and go to work in Manhattan in some of the ugliest buildings in the country, and yet they do not notice the ugliness, or they choose to ignore it. They are not reliable judges of the significance of their environment because they have not been trained to perceive the kind of meanings an environment implies.

If we assume that the perception of form is a human need, then the arts must play a crucial role in the education of every man, but the role will not be the one usually and most easily devised for the arts. That role was devised to introduce children and young men and women into a world where art is the ornament of genteel lives, or a good hedge against the market, or anything except an essential part of one's life. Our world is dominated by process rather than form, and will remain so until we recognize form when we see it.

Education must provide all students with some capacity for sensual perception and expression, with an understanding of the necessary interplay of perception and expression. The judgment of human creations obviously requires the ability to perceive different options. The student needs to know what the past can provide in the way of models of perception, and he will need to experiment with ways to perceive and ways to integrate his own perceptions. To the extent that he is aware of the continuity of his mode of seeing (or hearing, or touching, or reading) with that of other men, he will have a sense of rootedness in a tradition which he can accept as his own. But the mode of seeing must still be genuinely his. He will be the creator of his perception, and that means he must know what it means to create an object or event with artistry.

The importance of these fundamental principles extends beyond educational policy. If a fatalist is a person who has no faith in his own ability to direct his course and consequently submits to a course conceived elsewhere, then we have reared a nation of fatalists. It is ironic that this has happened in a nation usually thought of as "optimistic" and "future-oriented"—with its notion of manifest destiny and its adulation of productivity and progress—but that very orientation is at the root of the matter. Such goals cannot be phrased in terms of the individual human being, and men instinctively perceive their irrelevance to actually living out each day. Their promise of a future for an individual personality is illusory.

Time passes without shaping anything. Americans are producers of produce, and American consumers consume perishables. The myth of progress and production precludes the possibility of arrival. We have no eschatology, just escalation. Nor can we have until we have developed an art which allows each of us to reassert form upon time. We move from school to job to job, from farm to city to suburb, from house to house, and are not free. A college could help its students see the paradoxical relation between tradition and freedom if it were prepared to introduce a radically new kind of curriculum, administration, and faculty. Not to do so will make liberal education—the education of free men—a thing of the past.

Artist
and
University

ERIC LARRABEE

The preceding chapter, "The Humanities Museum," suggests that American affluence has bred a generation that is questioning the American way of life. Following this same thesis, Eric Larrabee, in this next chapter, "Artist and University," develops the point that the demand that grows out of such questioning is for a more livable world and that the need is for men and women who can effectively meet the challenge. He believes that although the need is obvious, educational institutions have not yet recognized it. Nor do they understand that the arts have come to be a necessity, not an ornament to be admired. For important reasons, therefore, he would put the arts on a par with other professional studies and nourish them as a necessary part of the educational environment.

Eric Larrabee is presently provost of the faculty of arts and letters at the State University of New York at Buffalo, and is involved in problems of higher education in the visual arts, music, theater, film, and literature. He studied painting technique at Harvard and was cartoonist, as well as writer, for the Harvard Lampoon. *For many years, as an editor of* Harper's, *he collaborated with Russell Lynes on a monthly column ("After Hours") about the arts and entertainments. He later became managing editor of* Horizon. *He is a member of the New York State Council on the Arts and the National Committee on the Humanities in the Schools, which during the past year has been involved in a review of humanities teaching at the high school level.*

At the time the formula "artist in residence" came into vogue, reputedly in the early 1930's when John Steuart Curry was invited to the University of Wisconsin and Paul Sample to Dartmouth, the term itself implied an unusual arrangement. The artist was to be located in an academic setting with some fanfare, calling attention to his merits and the university's courage in supporting them. Within a few years (stimulated by the Carnegie Corporation under President Frederick P. Keppel) the example was widely imitated, but there could still be debate on whether the idea of an artist in residence was a "success."

Today this concern seems very much of the past. Now the question is not so much whether individual artists can be at home in Academia but whether whole troupes of them can be stabled there—quartets, symphonies, operas, repertory theater groups, ballets. Rare are the institutions of higher learning with available space and a generous donor which have not constructed an Arts Center, and rarer still are those which do not consider a steady stream of local or visiting arts activities —plays, concerts, exhibitions, poetry readings—as normal and necessary components of university life. By all visible tokens, the arts have come to the campus to stay.

Initially they arrived in somewhat curious garb—that is, wearing whatever camouflage would permit them to survive in an alien environment. First to make the crossing were the poets, in good part because a number of them coincidentally were of scholarly bent and happened to espouse a highly intellectualized doctrine. Other arts, at least in the democratizing institutions west of the Alleghenies, often masqueraded as crafts and were taught in terms of technical accomplishment, the studio or conservatory approach, which in some fields is still today the only avenue to professional competence. But in general, if one may speak of recent and American experience, the arts were allowed to mingle with the established disciplines only after they had made themselves over into reasonable facsimiles of scholarship.

Art and music history were permissible because they had long been the object of that ferocious Germanic pedantry which had made *kunstgeschichtliche* such a richly connotative and frequently pejorative term. At its most exquisite—or more accurately, at Harvard—the ideal of art training at a university level was connoisseurship: an educative process intended to produce if not new Berensons then at least a steady stream of employable curators to staff the increasingly numerous and extensive American collections. In this rarefied atmosphere a living and performing painter would have seemed, and soon been made to feel, an obscenity.

Music has perhaps fared better, partly because a minimal capacity for performance (*i.e.* the ability to play the piano) was regarded as necessary, before the arrival of the long-playing record, for an acceptable comprehension of its literature. Singing in a chorus or playing in a brass band were of course unobjectionable in that they had become extracurricular, associated with student life after the Heidelberg light-opera model, and therefore devoid of any dangerously over-artistic implications. Composers were also regularly to be found on college faculties, though the reason may often have been—as the late Henry Cowell pointed out—that no serious composer could make a decent living from his music.

Theater, however, was on the borderline. Not that there was any denying drama its credentials; too many of its major works would have to be taught whether or not they could be performed, and there was after all only a fine line between the teaching of novel-writing and the teaching of play-writing, despite the fact that Harvard did manage to draw it and condemn George Pierce Baker to Yale. But actual presentation, merely of the standard plays at a professional level of skill, was something else again. In the first place it was expensive; the hazards of repertory have bankrupted more than one commercial company. Worse, it was distracting; it took up faculty and student time and energy to an extent that could well be criticized as educationally out of proportion to its worth. Academic theater has survived, and occasionally flourished, but powerful personalities and no little exertion have been needed to keep it going—and, even in the new dispensation of presumed artistic affluence, many of its dilemmas persist.

At the heart of the matter was and is the living artist, a creature of problematical character. Where he wants to live and work may well depend on seemingly whimsical or paradoxical factors which offer little guidance: E. B. White prefers to write in hotel rooms, the sculptor David Smith chose to work at Bolton Landing—there is no predicting. But to locate the artist in an academic context is to place him in a structured relationship, and one for which he may have no affection. Scholars are implicitly his critics, and he theirs. When the subject at issue is art, the artist is a standing rebuke to the non-artist; even with the greatest of tact, which he has little incentive to cultivate, the artist must express something of his contempt for his parasite, the scholar, simply in order to exist as a creative organism. Robert Frost was a fully representative artist in residence, precisely because of his lover's quarrel with Academe; he could live neither with it nor away from it.

There is much to be said for maintaining a strict and hygienic separation. To put the artist on display is to make him self-conscious, in the worst sense—to embed him in the notion of the artist as curiosity. He is being valued not for his work as an end product, but for himself as a spectacle in the act of creating it; otherwise there would be no need for him to be present. His presence is being asked to convey virtue to his surroundings, as though there were—as in truth there are—magical properties in his "art." He becomes a shaman, willingly or not, and is believed to be flawed as the shaman is flawed through having survived exposure to something terrifying and unfathomable. He is all at once an oddity, a tame pet, a demonstration model, and a scapular against the Philistines; it is a wonder he survives at all the encounter with a smothering embrace from those explicators and evaluators who must always be, as in moments of sanity he knows, his natural enemies.

But what of the contrary view? Artists are drawn to Academia much as they are drawn to "artists' colonies," and for many of the same reasons. First among them is undoubtedly the lure of economic security, the promise of surcease, however temporary, from those anxieties over mere physical survival which appear to have ravaged the artistic personality ever since it became aware of itself. The promise is illusory, but no matter; the artist of all people knows that nothing is bought without cost, but this particular purchase—the reassuring sensation that society, if only for a moment, is willing to support him just for being himself— is one that many artists will willingly make. A close-second reason, and a supplement to the sense of being "wanted," is the ambiguous appeal of living among like-minded people, of belonging to a community in which one's own values are held in high esteem. Here also there is both attraction and repulsion; the ego inevitably pays a price for being in the presence of too many other egos.

From the university's side, on the other hand, the gains are more apparent. At least within the liberal-arts inheritance the artist is the primary resource, a living witness to the vitality of the humanistic enterprise. If that mound of words and artifacts called "the humanities" is of worth, then worthier still are the creative acts from which it emerged, and even more so those present-day creators who validate the tradition. The universities' role, viewed in contrast, is essentially custodial.

The scholar must accept a subsidiary place in much the same way that Freud would have even the psychoanalyst bow, when the question is finally faced, before the mystery of art's birth. But it need not denigrate the scholar to think of him as a kind of ultimate critic; the so-called verdict of generations, which confers the status of classic on a given work, is commonly the verdict of generations of scholars. The function of an artist in a nest of critics is therefore equally classical: to keep them honest.

This primacy of the "creative" has elements of the fashionable, to be sure, as the myth holds it to have had in American education, since John Dewey. Fiction is supposed to be more creative than nonfiction; poetry more creative than prose; abstract expressionism more creative than the dutiful representation of the human anatomy. Everybody knows these things; they are part of revealed truth. But if it is clearly the case, for example, that the "progressive" Dewey, whose name is used to frighten voters into disapproving school bond issues, is a chimera, then equally is it clear—from the numerous current accounts of what actually goes on in American high schools—that the emphasis on creativity is being damned too soon, before it has had any real impact on the secondary-school teaching of the humanities, which is still as much a matter of rote and formula as it ever was. Patience is recommended, in other words, in dealing with the more absurd manifestations of "self-expression" as an educational aim. There is something residually sound in the notion that it is inherently admirable to make an entity which never existed before—something sound, similarly, in the notion that a scholar earns his license to practice by contributing to the heritage he exploits, by adding his little fragment to the sum total of knowledge.

The American ideal of the university, attempting as it does to have the best of all previous worlds, presumes to embody both British collegiality and German institutionalized research. In the American version this has come to mean that first-rate departments and first-rate scholars are "productive," in the sense that they pursue scholarly inquiry and publish its results, with all the familiar consequences in terms of tension between the often-neglected craft of teaching and the lengthening list of citations on which honor and promotion depend. But the tension is, or should be, fruitful. The pressure to be productive is pressure to remain alive, and while the standard based on publication may be less than perfect, it operates as often to keep departments lean and muscular as it does to punish a gifted teacher who happens not to publish. At any event, the pull of cross-purposes is probably overstressed; what matters here is the implication for the arts, specifically: What is the artistic analogue to research?

Perhaps the question can best be answered by a comparison with another field. In medicine, the education of doctors as we know it has developed over several hundred years. By the middle of the eighteenth century a method based on the teaching hospital had been worked out which still persists, with little change, today. For example, an institution like The New York Hospital had its origin (1771) in a single speech delivered by Samuel Bard, a twenty-eight-year-old New York physician just returned from taking his degree at Edinburgh. Bard spelled out the three purposes he believed a teaching hospital should have: the care of patients, the training of future physicians, and the study of the causes of disease. By combining practice, teaching, and research, medicine transformed itself, as the arts are being called upon to transform themselves now. The difficulty is that the arts, by the same token, are not even at the stage which medicine had reached in 1770. It is rare in the arts to find a university department with a balanced threefold capability; the best of them gladly settle for two, and a depressingly large number must be content with one alone. Rarer still are the men who accept more than one of the three missions as their own responsibility. The artist-teacher, or the teacher-scholar, is sufficiently unusual to be high in demand, the darling of administrators hungry for talent. The artist-teacher-scholar is almost nonexistent.

What one means by saying that a certain type does not exist, is that living people who exemplify it do not come forward. Society has not demanded that they fill that particular role, while it permits other and lesser roles to be regarded as adequate—for example, the role of an art professor who was a promising painter when he achieved tenure but has since rotted away in the company of students so inert that he has come to resemble a Racine scholar teaching elementary French. The first-rate —or at least the visibly and successfully first-rate—do not need the university as a refuge, with the result that some artists on campuses may turn out to be there because they can't survive anywhere else. "I'd be excited about doing a joint course with a painter," one distinguished art historian has remarked, "if the painters in my college were as stimulating as the ones I know outside."

What is needed, therefore, is that most difficult exercise: the invention of new social roles. It is by no means easy for academic doctors to be simultaneously teachers, researchers, and clinicians, but they all make a stab at it, even when they know themselves to be woefully inadequate in one or another capacity, because they have been persuaded that the three-cornered model is a desirable and necessary ideal. Undoubtedly it is now true that many artists would make bad teachers, and many more scholars would make bad artists, but we should be able to admit that fact without having to accept it as final.

The obligation of the arts to transform themselves is imposed by society, but it falls upon the universities with special force. Staffing revolutions—that is, training the agents of social change—is one of higher education's immemorial functions, but what is happening to the arts is now happening faster than universities have made allowance for. American hyperbole has labeled the event "cultural explosion," so the term must be immediately qualified, but no matter how skeptical one may be about the meaning of quantitative indices, the figures attest to the transitions from a class to a mass phenomenon—from cult to culture, as Alvin Toffler put it in *The Culture Consumers* (1964). "The rise of a mass public for the arts," wrote Mr. Toffler, giving numerous examples, "can, in its way, be compared with the rise of mass literacy in the eighteenth century in England." Money spent, money donated, number of persons producing or consuming—all have been rising at a rate so much faster than population growth that the arts, viewed purely as a business enterprise, are now among the major industries. Most artists still starve, to be sure, but they starve now on a nationally recognized scale; their monetary plight is learnedly studied and deplored, surely a sign that they are about to arrive at economic maturity.

Behind the statistical increase in activity is the far more fundamental fact it reflects: The arts have become necessary. Hitherto they may have been vital, a deep reflex of the human condition, an ornament to man's tenancy on his planet, or what-have-you, but they could never be included—as the twentieth century requires them to be—among the necessary conditions of survival. Man must now either learn to live aesthetically or cease to be man—cease to be, that is, an animal who responds meaningfully to challenge.

The phenomenon of the twentieth century is the significant increase in the power of individuals to affect their environment and one another. The world was manageable, aesthetically and otherwise, as long as only a small number of people could disturb the public order; that order has got out of hand, on every side, in proportion to the added number of voices which cry to be heard, the number of interests which can effectively demand to be recognized. The process cannot be reversed. In every field the dilemma is the same—essentially a federal one: how to reconcile divergent interests with the common good. One by one the challenges have been faced, and allowing for a century or two leeway, overcome. Everyone has had to become a citizen; everyone must soon become economically self-sufficient. Just so must everyone someday become an artist—or a saint. On or back we must go—as C. S. Lewis once wrote—to stay here is death.

Another way of putting it—and a time-worn phrasing ever since John Adams made that endlessly quotable remark about studying war so that his sons could study commerce so that *their* sons could study the arts—is to say that American society, having solved the problems of political and economic democracy, must now solve those of aesthetic democracy. At each stage there have been ample grounds for believing that a majority of the people could not be trusted; certainly there are reasons enough to doubt that even the present degree of democratization in aesthetic decision-making can ever produce anything but the present result, which is the lowest common denominator of mass taste, kinetic chaos in the environment, and bankruptcy for the artist. The very suggestion that taste can be trained, or at least that trained taste has some advantage over untrained, would undoubtedy be damned as elitist and slightly smelling of artistic fascism if it were seriously to be advanced. On or back we must go; there is no way ahead but straight forward, to take a chance on aesthetic democracy and try to prepare people, in very large numbers, to make aesthetic decisions responsibly and well.

If the more affluent we become, the more members there are of every generation who are dissatisfied, then the one thing they seem able to agree on being dissatisfied about is the unlivable, uninhabitable nature of the world which material affluence has provided for them. Curiously enough, this is simultaneously an affirmation and a denial of the Protestant Ethic—an affirmation in the sense that selfish protest is exactly the kind of work the devil could be expected to find for idle hands to do, but a denial in the sense that surfeit has brought no relaxation into apathy. The puritan nightmare about prosperity was that if no one had to work, no one would; the fiber would go out of the national character. Dissatisfaction with one's lot was thought to be the fuel not only of the bourgeois upward-mobility machine, the little wheel which kept society's big wheels turning, but of the long tradition of left-socialist agitation which brought about reforms to make prosperity general and by and large humane. Some other kind of dissatisfaction, fueling protest of a wholly different kind, would have seemed unthinkable a generation ago to conservatives and radicals alike, as to many of them it still does.

Admittedly, the pervasive discontent of the present period is as likely to reflect itself in escape—the flight from reality into "beautiful" experience—as in programmatic reform. The positive energies of the young radicals are directed against war, poverty, prejudice; they are political and highly moral, if not puritanical. But they have disconnected themselves from the utilitarian model of society. They deny economic man; they announce Daniel Bell's post-industrial man, and not a few of them have arrived at Bell's end of ideology. They ask for the imposition of a

48

completely different set of standards than industrial-democratic-liberal society had hitherto presupposed.

State it, if you like, in the form of a law: Under conditions of affluence dissatisfaction focuses on the quality of life. Anxieties are diffuse, demands are contradictory; there is a sense of aimlessness, as though we had come loose from old moorings and no new ones were in sight. To worry about the state of one's immortal soul is doubtless a luxury (as the Church has recognized by the judicious handling of its contemplatives) but it is a luxury which increasing multitudes can afford —in fact, cannot escape. In conditions of scarcity the "cultural" questions simply do not come up: What to do with time, how to make life meaningful, where to turn for pleasure and peace. But once raised, under affluence, they clamor to be answered, and a society which persistently asks itself questions which it does not answer will accumulate dissatisfactions at a prodigious rate. Under affluence, to state the law's corollary, the arts become necessary.

It is in the light of this imperative that the place of the arts and the artist in a university setting must be viewed. If one begins simply by asking an educational question, or by challenging the relevance of the arts in an all-too-painfully obvious educational crisis, then the argument will be endless; there is no "justification" for art in such a context or, at best, only a weak and defensive one. But if one begins with a societal demand, with a felt and explicit need for which no other answer exists, then the obligation of universities to restructure and fortify their commitment to the arts will emerge forthwith.

Partly this is a matter of talking the traditional language of educators; professional training of any kind can always be pushed forward by political pressure from the constituency which hungers for its products and, in effect, guarantees them jobs. In the past, not to belabor the point, the arts have suffered in proportion to their inability to demonstrate that jobs exist, or even ought to exist. Therefore one should not underestimate the importance, in this respect, of findings like those of the Rockefeller Brothers Special Fund report on the performing arts: that many arts organizations suffer more from a lack of managerial talent than of the other, more obvious, resources—and the further report (prepared for the New York State Council on the Arts by George Alan Smith) which shows that in the next five years over two hundred positions in arts administration, with combined salaries of over two million dollars, will fall open in New York State alone.

What the universities need badly to realize, and so patently do not, is that the country as a whole is far ahead of them in making the arts integral to the socio-economic process. In his speech to the annual meeting of governors in 1967, Governor Rockefeller used Syracuse (population: 212,000), which surely can be called an average community, as an example of the current expansion of the arts as purely economic activities. During the 1966 season in Syracuse, the arts outdrew baseball five to one; 583 arts programs were presented in 906 performances; approximately one-twelfth of the population was engaged in producing arts events, for which the audience was nine times greater than the total attendance at all conventions, conferences, and trade shows, and for which the minimal cash outlay was more than $2.5 million. Between 1960 and 1965 the number of arts organizations in Syracuse increased from twenty-eight to fifty-one (or 82 per cent), while the total number of arts programs increased 87 per cent. This, as the Governor went on to emphasize, is the characteristic pattern throughout the country. During 1966 alone some three hundred new arts organizations were formed and given tax-exempt status.

Today we are the possessors, for better or worse, of an educational system which is professionally oriented. The guidance offered students, and the machinery of regulations with which they must cope, offers them every encouragement to direct themselves toward narrow, utilitarian goals, and away from the pattern of humanistic "general education" in which the arts were at least tolerated, if not much more. It is a common suspicion that, were all such restrictions removed, many more students would opt for the arts than presently do, adding still another distortion to the background of reality behind our immediate concern. Perhaps liberal education can still be saved (it has many secret admirers, and a hard-core underground of those who never abandoned it anyhow) but for the near future there is much to be said for playing the game by the existing rules—that is, for defending the arts by professionalizing them, by basing them as other professions have been based in advanced university training, and by nourishing their scholarly and intellectual substance to match that of other disciplines.

For long there has been a tendency in the arts to assume that amateurism and an easygoing economic laissez-faire were virtues or, worse, somehow necessary to the artist's integrity and self-respect. This assumption is now doing material damage, and the time has long since arrived when it should seriously be questioned. No great association with present-day arts organizations is needed to convince anyone that the plague of amateurism is widespread; one need intend no injury to the decent, dedicated people involved by saying that many of them are in over their depth, helplessly buffeted by forces they can neither understand nor control. We need trained people. Universities are where people are trained. Q. E. D.

At the same time, we find ourselves at a moment in time when much of higher education—at least in its undergraduate component—is up for grabs. There is a widespread uncertainty, not only about its traditional methods, but about their purpose. What, effectively, is the student preparing *for*? Since no one any longer knows, there is everywhere in Academia a liberalizing mood, a trend toward loosening the bonds, breaking the lock-step patterns, multiplying the possible paths toward a degree. If these numerous, sometimes radical and sometimes curiously tentative, moves have anything in common, it is their acceptance of self-realization on the undergraduate's part as the only legitimate but sufficiently comprehensive aim. If this is to become the general pattern, then a startling growth in university arts programs is not merely probable but inevitable, for the realization of human potentiality is all at once their subject matter, their method, and their goal.

Perhaps it is at this point that a useful distinction can be made between art and art education. Obviously one can be educated in art without being an artist. The training of sensibility—that is, the exercise and refinement of the sensuous powers—is not only possible for a vastly larger number of people than can themselves create art, but serves to bring about a social climate favorable to artistic flowering. Great artists, as Walt Whitman said, need great audiences to nurture them. If one imagines what such a society might be like, granting the effort required, then it becomes far easier to visualize the university as that society in microcosm—a condensed and exemplary expression of how life might be lived at a high pitch of aesthetic awareness. For such a university would also be permeated with that spirit and style in which Aldous Huxley remarked that the greatest of the arts is living.

The Artist as Teacher

ROBERT WATTS

> *Most teaching in the visual arts,
> Robert Watts states in the following chapter, "The Artist as Teacher,"
> neither takes into account what art is all about nor what students are
> concerned about. He believes that real changes, not tokenism, are
> required to work out these issues. Along with Eric Larrabee, in the fore-
> going chapter, he would like to see the arts treated as equal to other
> study areas, and he proposes ways in which this might be fostered. His*

goal would be to set up a college environment where the arts would be encouraged to develop and where flexibility would be the rule.

An engineer and an artist, Robert Watts is also an historian with a special interest in primitive art. In his own work he explores the possibilities of technology, seeing new dimensions—and often amusing ones —in the machine, adapting light and experimenting with sound to create new environments. He is a member of the Fluxus Group and of the board of directors of Fluxhouse Cooperatives for Artists, New York City. Presently associate professor at Rutgers University, he was on leave in 1968-69 to be a member of a special study group at the University of California, Santa Cruz.

André Breton once said the man who cannot visualize a horse galloping on a tomato is an idiot.

Man and His Symbols by Carl Jung

The artist is the man in any field, scientific or humanistic, who grasps the implications of his actions and of new knowledge in his own time. He is the man of integral awareness.

Understanding Media by Marshall McLuhan

In listening to students talk about what they would like to have, as opposed to what they are getting, it has become apparent that the gap is considerable. The college student is in search of ways to relate to the world. He is asking for courses that will help him comprehend the complexities of contemporary life in an age of advanced technology. He wants to know how to deal realistically with the condition of mankind at this moment in this place.

I believe that it is in this area that colleges have been most neglectful, and that it is in this area the arts as well as the sciences can be made most relevant.

No college should claim to be educating young people unless it exposes them to the nature of the ills of our society and attempts to give them, at the same time, a firm grasp of the nature of man and his world and a personal desire to explore, to invent, even to create, and to change oneself as well as the world. This kind of education requires a responsible and responsive give-and-take that is non-existent in most classrooms and lecture halls.

It is my belief that if students are to find something in art that is relevant to their concerns they will need both help and encouragement. To get an exact awareness of the real nature of creative problems, they can investigate for themselves the newer movements in art: new music, non-music, time, space, light, optics, junk art, kinetic art, still photography, moving pictures, the "silence" of John Cage, the environment, the happening, the event—and related aspects of the physical and the man-made world: plants, water, synthetic food. It is the job of the artist-teacher to participate in discussion and analysis of student work and ideas growing out of such study, in relation to the student himself, to his attitudes and goals, and to the history of art and contemporary art problems. Through such a process a student becomes capable of expanding his knowledge to the real issues of the day and further, if he wishes, to the experimental ideas at work in the contemporary art scene.

Creative experience combined with historical study can help students to fill two needs: a sense of history (and one's place in it) and a sense of community (of art as communal as well as individual endeavor). Neither sense can be developed solely by the lecturer or imbibed from any book, and the artist-teacher therefore can be important at certain points in helping to "hook" students on the need to build these foundations themselves. To do this, the emphasis in an art studio situation should be on learning rather than on teaching. Just as the lecture cannot get this across, neither can the assignment of a mass problem to be solved in a set period of time. The dreary and meaningless works that come out of such assignments affirm the inadequacy of that method.

The bulk of our artistic tradition has been the production of object art. We build museums to house objects; we train people to produce objects. Yet from contemporary life we are learning that artistic experience is possible in other than sheer object form. Students who have been freed by (or from) the curriculum to explore these other possibilities are learning and producing new forms. One student I know who was in her third year, painting bad pictures and doing worse drawings, started to work with "light" in her own fashion and following her own ideas.

She began with simple experiments, filling jugs with colored liquids and suspending assorted reflective and transparent materials and objects within the jars on nylon cords. Now, she is exploring "light" and "no light," is arranging events for a theater, and is collaborating with a young composer on new musical works.

Another, who became interested in ideas about randomness and chance operations—"I see the world as a place of chanceful change"— worked on an environmental box which successfully contrasted fixed and changing worlds. He manufactured by hand most of the things that could be bought.

Teaching art is a process that is generally not well understood. If it were sufficiently known that the creative process is in delicate balance when it functions well, that it is altogether miraculous when anything comes of it in an institutional setting, only then perhaps could we expect educators to provide the conditions under which the arts may be explored. This does not mean physical or philosophical separation from the rest of the college or university but, on the contrary, integration and acceptance of art study as part of the educational process open to all students.

More importantly, however, the people responsible for art programs —whether administrators or professors—must become aware of the exacting demands of the process of creation itself and receptive to the changing art ambiance. Artist-teachers must insist that conditions for art in the classroom more closely approach those for art in the real world and private studio, and abandon the traditional art classroom for a more favorable environment. Student artists have approximately the same needs as artist-teachers, and their day-to-day encounters with art problems are the same.

One can imagine situations where the resources of the institution, informational and technological, could provide what is now needed for newer explorations in art. Indeed, these resources are perhaps the most valuable contribution of a university—perhaps the best reason for putting the arts into the college curriculum. Art workshops equipped with modern technology must be made available to student artists, and students must move from one area to another as the creative process demands. This means access to technical guidance as well as to equipment, cameras, recorders, computers. Proper instruction in the fields where this technology is applied is essential. A truly exploratory atmosphere, a real learning experience, must be substituted for the conventional teaching experience where non-existent principles of art are wrongly postulated as absolutes to student artists.

One must realize that art is deeply connected with the basic drives for communication and personal expression and suffers at the hands of authoritarians or dogmatists who feel that they know best.

At some colleges and among some teachers I sense a bias that art is not for everyone. How do colleges decide how much art to teach to how many people? I don't think they know what should be taught to whom but they seem to presume that they do. Instead, they should assume that there may be different kinds of art and art training for different kinds of people, depending on what their major activity is going to be, and that everybody needs some sort of experience with art or some kind of acquaintance with it. One way to go about deciding what has to be taught and what is to be learned is to ask students, and to provide opportunities for considering and trying out what they say they would like to have. This is much better for the non-major than having a higher authority state, "Now, general student, this is what you need to know about art, and this is what will make you happy and will keep you from being frustrated in your old age." And it's still better for the potential arts major, who would thus see real interchange at work.

A major question that seems to concern most colleges is how you can teach a great many art students economically, the way it's presumed that you can teach other knowledge to large numbers of students. If the problem is posed in terms of large numbers of students, then I propose that college art faculties begin to work with mass media and self-teaching techniques to satisfy some aspects of their problem and to gain time and money to deal more intensively with smaller groups of students in other situations.

But the artist-teachers and historians also need to think in terms of alternatives for handling different kinds of students beyond the accepted system for lecturing or mass studio situations. There must be a variety of ways of doing the job with large numbers of young students, as well as with smaller groups and with adults who are coming back to college wanting the kind of art training they were deprived of in the early part of their lives. We can deal with these problems if we are free and loose enough to experiment.

To experiment with the whole student body of the college, introductory art on closed-circuit TV could be shown three times a day, at certain specified times. The students would know that they could get it when they want it, and maybe that's enough. For students who want credit, an examination could be required at the end, and graded. I think we have to relax our regulations and try all kinds of experiments to see what really works.

However, it is not enough to transfer an ordinary art history course into the television medium, because simple transfer will not work and students will not accept it. Television must be used by persons who can combine knowledge of content with understanding of camera techniques. Its particular requirements must be met by any course planner who attempts to convey the sense of art by this means.

I would insist that the people who handle the introductory art history materials be very special people. They must know what questions to raise, and encourage students to pose the problems. I would say that it is this kind of person we must train for the future of art education. They are not the traditional art historians; they need much more than historical research capabilities. They need perspective and vision in respect to the past, the present, and the future, and in addition they must know how artists go about their work, how they make their decisions, and how they discard or revive theories as well as invent.

To experiment with studio instruction a network of workshops could be organized primarily for the younger students—perhaps combining them with adults who have an awakened interest in art. Sessions might be in the afternoon and evening hours when the needed spaces could be found to allow for as many workshops as possible. Would-be artist-teachers, or art students who are curious about the teaching-learning process, could run these workshops under objectives set jointly with faculty. The student teachers might get credit toward their degree. Students and adults in the workshops would not necessarily receive grades, but the hours spent could be written down in their academic records. Within such a class, there might be students who are beginning their study in art—their probable major—but the overwhelming number would just want to create something. Everyone is studying and, although their goals are different, ultimately they are reconciled if a vital learning situation is realized. All in the workshops are interested in making art and all are producing.

In such situations we are coping with a mixture of students, those who are art majors, those who are not, as well as persons enrolled in adult education programs who often have a special concern or need. Some students have only a passing interest, because the work is an elective and it may be a chance to take something for credit that looks easy. I would accept this, and I would try to provide for all comers a stimulating and challenging experience which would provoke a genuine involvement.

The college's problems are deeper when the concern is for handling the serious art students who hope to be artists or art teachers. Loosening up the academic situation as I have suggested will help to solve some of the problems of who's going to get what kind of instruction, but artists and historians teaching in colleges need to think about other related problems. They must step out of the ivory tower to consider some of the things that students face in deciding to major, or even to take courses in an art field. The most basic problem for students is deciding on the relative importance of the arts experience in their higher education. This can be answered in part for them if course content is presented in contemporary terms. For the students who have an interest in art but do not see a career line, there is need for faculty guidance. New options need to be developed for such students other than the standard ones of artist, teacher, or research historian. Some new possibilities include management roles in museums, art centers, and in college and university art programs. They could fill positions that are usually given to untrained and underpaid staff when the jobs actually rate more, both in pay and in background. Art faculties could help to train such people as well as hire them. They could also show art majors that the goal of aspiring to be a first-, second- or even third-rate artist or historian is not realistic but that persons trained in art can work successfully in many situations, bringing interest and energy to jobs that need them. Schools and such community programs as Upward Bound, Head Start, VISTA and the Peace Corps need staff who have a sense of the creative process. While in college, students could have field experience in some of these programs and receive credit. This type of activity could demonstrate to both students and administrators the relevance of the arts to the contemporary world.

Special space will be needed to provide the type of unique art situation discussed here, with access to technological advice and with expanded library and information resources. Students and staff need places where they can carry on their own work without the interruption of incoming classes or the constraints of dormitory space. In many instances there are undoubtedly existing spaces that would be adequate for such use if the administration did not feel that the buildings were too old and not worth simple repairs. Artists like such space and prefer it to sterile, non-useful, contemporary buildings; but to make this point, art faculties will have to be more aggressive and more determined in getting across the nature of the job that they want to do.

Artist-teachers, art historians, and art students together must be given the permission (or be forced) to experiment in serious ways with facilities, the curriculum, scheduling courses, and loads. It is from this combination of artist, student, and historian that the college can learn what art it should try to teach, how it can be learned, where it should be taught, and how much of it can be taught at any one time. An unsympathetic and ignorant faculty or administration cannot legislate the needs and requirements for art teaching. It has been my experience that administrators are not especially informed about the arts and that they lack even elementary curiosity about these various fields. It should be some solace for college administrators, however, to have me admit that even among artists and teachers there are disagreements and uncertainties about teaching art, and they can be sure that an art department, just as any other department, can stagnate for a variety of reasons.

I think in many colleges the arts faculties are demoralized, and certain innovations might get positive responses from these faculties. Setting up an interdisciplinary committee on art could be a useful innovation for several reasons. If artists and historians could function within a small interdisciplinary committee, I believe that this would greatly enhance their status within the college and university. They would become personally better known and their contributions would be made more widely known to the whole college community. Any faculty group needs to think that what it is doing is very important, and I believe that all of its members need to feel this individually. If they have a sense of that importance, the present staff in certain colleges could initiate interesting innovations in teaching, although in other places arts people from the outside might have to be brought in to help stimulate change.

Departments, especially at the undergraduate level, perhaps at the graduate level, could be disbanded and administrative needs such as hiring, firing, salary reviews, handled centrally. The committee system is one possible way to organize, and to find new means to new learning situations.

I am not sure what the results would be, but combining the artist with a biologist, a psychologist, a sociologist, and a philosopher in an interdisciplinary arts committee could generate ideas. It could be that the biologist would be invited into the arts classroom to talk about the structure of plants, or molecular structure; or the psychologist would be asked to discuss his understanding of visual perception and the creative process.

Within an interdisciplinary group the first question would be: What should we be teaching? It is basic questions such as this which are not being asked and are not being dealt with, on the seeming assumption that we already have faced them—yet it is in the areas of life where we make such assumptions that we do not really know very much.

The experimentation that needs to occur is operational on several levels and in all instances should be in the context of the particular institution with its special history, geography, personnel, and facilities. It must be ascertained realistically what is special and unique about a particular place and time, what local ingredients make change possible or needed. The climate for art will not be the same for Topeka as for Chicago or Newtown, but in any college the arts faculty together with the college as a whole could do far more than is now done to evolve programs and situations with special significance for their own institutions, ever mindful of what is happening elsewhere. Much more could also be done to expose students to other centers of art, perhaps on some exchange basis. Despite what administrators may say, there is no reason to expect that doing something different will cost more. It becomes a problem of priority. It is not a question of throwing out the old for the unknown benefits of a new approach but of setting up an environment where faculty and students, with the administration, can work together for the right change, re-shaping curriculum, changing priorities.

Most college goals are wrong for students. What does education in the arts mean for a student? Why should he want art experience? These are valid questions for both non-majors and majors, questions which they should be asking before they enter the classroom, and which should be asked of them by a responsible faculty.

The goals of the arts faculty are also wrong. And for this reason the wrong artists may be attracted to teaching positions. The goals should not be to instruct in one method or approach or to try to instill a set of personal theories, but to encourage students to study by opening up the possibilities for creative exploration and working with each student as he struggles to realize his own potential gifts, artistic or otherwise. The artist-teacher cannot seek these goals unless he has some prerogatives. Teaching loads must be adjustable and not subjected to arbitrary student-faculty ratios. Every learning situation must be considered something special and structured in size to allow maximum interchange. The artist-teacher must also be provided with time for his own creative work and research, to assure that he maintains his momentum for teaching.

Recently I was on the Santa Cruz campus of the University of California as one of three teachers in a special program to see how a vital visual experience can evolve. The students were a mix of undergraduate majors and non-majors, of all backgrounds, ages, and collegiate levels. The staff for this special program consisted of a cultural anthropologist who is a communications man, an art historian who is particularly interested in the twentieth century, and a practicing artist who is also a teacher. There were three "new courses": a large lecture for over 300, on contemporary issues ranging over the social, economic, cultural and communication problems of today (this was taught by the anthropologist); a seminar for about 20 students on the topic of modern times (this was carried by the art historian); and my own experimental workshop in mixed media. No attempt was made to interrelate closely what was being taught in the three projects but each of the three "courses" or projects was considered part of a whole with the aim of designing learning situations that could benefit all kinds of students who might be interested in the visual world and in communicating their interest.

A deliberate effort was made to bring in outside points of view by inviting guests from all forms of art, including dance, music, film, theater, architecture, planning. These guests talked to the university community and to smaller groups of students and teachers about their art, their ideas on art, and their thoughts about the teaching of art. Sound tapes of these discussions were available to all students day or night through a dialing system provided by the university.

Students were expected to become aware and responsible for their actions; to read as well as observe; and to develop their critical senses. In each of the three "courses" they were not "given" ideas, but rather led to develop their own. This was reinforcement which helped students do their own correlation of the material in the three projects, and even if a student was not involved in all three he got an idea from his fellow students as to what went on in the ones he had missed. This active exchange of experience and knowledge, encouraged by the teaching situation, is not a simple process.

In my workshop, for example, eight weeks were needed to form a group of ten students who eventually produced a "performance evening" on their own, with complete responsibility. The eight weeks were spent in testing out performance ideas on site (in this case, out of doors) and under all conditions of light, time, weather, and so forth. Not until the fifth week did one student finally feel strong enough to act as leader or director for the anticipated performance. While I had only a few students enrolled in this workshop, many more came in and out to observe, and I spent hours with even more in conversations about the nature of art and of man.

The side effects from this kind of program are many. Students in the large lecture group became aware of what was happening in the seminar and the workshop, and began to drift in. They wanted to make a film or learn something about taking pictures or work in the darkroom. They may have had a camera but may never have learned to use it; now they seemed to want to learn. Students from the seminar got an idea which they came to the workshop to try out—"What would happen if this tape were put through more than one machine at a time? Could I mix in something else—other sounds?" Students who had previously deserted painting because they found they had nothing to "say" returned to it with apparent enthusiasm. Others who had been flying balloons and kites they had designed got local children to join them on Saturday afternoons—and they began some interesting and important exchanges of ideas and experiences with these children.

Students said that they had gone through an exciting and stimulating learning experience. They found it a challenge to relate varied points of view, and they carried on questioning periods outside the regular school day. One experience seemed to lead to another, with students seeking out answers on complicated problems in communications, aided by easy access to books and other writing, to versatile materials and equipment, and to the newest technology. The students kept coming back for more, and Santa Cruz's permanent staff in painting and sculpture began talking about their gains from the program in their own teaching. What we had apparently achieved was a true interaction between students and teachers, and what I would call a vital enterprise of learning.

Education
of
Vision

JAMES ACKERMAN

> *To achieve the kind of setting that Robert Watts, in his chapter "The Artist as Teacher," pictures as essential for a visual arts program at a college will require the extensive changes in the philosophy of teaching that James Ackerman proposes in this chapter, "Education of Vision." He deals with various problems but stresses that it is the discipline, not the creative impulse, that must be emphasized in the arts. His specific ideas for stimulating teachers and*

engaging students are offered as a guide to colleges that are prepared to consider a new curriculum approach in the visual arts.

James Ackerman's teaching career began at Yale as a lecturer; later he went to the University of California at Berkeley; and then to Harvard where he is now a professor and served as head of the department of fine arts from 1963 to 1968. He has been a research fellow at the Council on the Humanities at Princeton, and under its auspices wrote, with Rhys Carpenter, the book Art and Archaeology. *He has received special awards for another book,* The Architecture of Michelangelo. *His latest publications have dealt with Andrea Palladio. During the last year and a half he has been chairman of a study group on the arts and humanities for the American Academy of Arts and Sciences, and is editor of the issue of the Academy's publication* Daedalus *that was devoted to "The Future of the Humanities."*

American intellectuals don't care for ideologies or even for theories; our attitudes and approaches are formed by prevailing *styles* rather than by articulated principles. Changes of position are not prompted by rational attempts at reform but by the tensions between incompatible styles.

At this moment the tension is mounting between the established style, which I shall call *Objective Analysis,* representing the intellectual achievement and position of the first half of the twentieth century, and the upstart style of *Engagement,* which is easiest to identify in the search by young people for new sensations and experiences, the mistrust of authority and tradition, and the eagerness to bear witness to strongly felt convictions.

Our present system of higher education has been developed to produce young people trained in the arts of analysis. It assumes that the primary responsibility of the scientist, scholar or artist is to his subject and craft, that the researcher should examine his material as objectively and impersonally as possible in order to minimize the danger that his point of view might distort the interpretation of it, and that the artist should be committed to the abstract imperatives of his craft, whether it be the authority of the picture plane for the painter or of a serial system for the composer. To have a point of view at all is considered an unscientific position unless it can be shown to be the result rather than the stimulus of investigation; "unscientific" because the educational theory of the last generation was haunted by a scientific image—a distorted image that represented science in the limited sense of dissection, measurement and testing.

Because the style of analysis demands an objective and impersonal relationship between the observer and the object of observation, it offers no way for learning and education to contribute to the formation or articulation of feelings and beliefs. It has produced a high standard of precision and of critical technique that has supported an age of great material progress, but it has not helped or even encouraged students to make social, political or aesthetic judgments.

The Engaged style cannot be defined clearly in these terms because it opposes not only the method of analysis but the concept of an articulated method itself. It is concerned with the absorption of experience rather than with its systematization, with input rather than output. It is individualist, vigorous in its opposition to prevailing systems and to the power that objective analysis has given to those who practice it. Its strength is one of antithesis, calling to attention the values that were considered irrelevant and damaging to the method of the opposition. In the form of student activism, it is making itself felt as a force in education through criticism of administrative regulations, of the academic authority and standards of faculties, and of curricula and teaching that lack "relevance" to contemporary life and issues.

Criticism from this source now is forcing a reassessment of the methods of objective analysis. It is becoming clear that our attempts to approximate objectivity—a condition that psychologists long ago demonstrated to be unattainable—keeps us from recognizing and examining the beliefs and principles by which we work, and promotes a professional training primarily devoted to method rather than to the study and formulation of principles and standards.

Although the style of Engagement has helped to reveal flaws in the dominant system, it is not by its nature equipped to provide alternatives applicable to a reform of education and scholarship. If the student or scholar were to replace his posture of objectivity with one of subjectivity, then investigation would become a process of casting onto the object the values and convictions he already possessed, and learning would be replaced by confirming. If, in the name of relevance, the criterion for the choice of objects of study were to become their applicability to immediate concerns, then the vast store of experience that is potentially but not immediately serviceable would be lost. Moreover, the individual whose predilections prompt him to constrict the potential sources of his experience is certain to hamper his capacity to cope even with the issues that most concern him.

The intensely felt convictions of the engaged student cannot have been formed in the books and classrooms of the analytic professors; they must have been absorbed from childhood on, out of the traditional homilies of American culture. Passionate feelings about liberty, equality, freedom, fair play, individuality, and so on, affect political and social attitudes and actions more than sober analysis and statistical research. But these commonly held ideals that help to bind our country together also cause divisive conflicts because they can appear to be incompatible (individualism versus the sharing of goods; loyalty to one's country versus the brotherhood of man). Having provided no means in our educational system for mediating between passions and thought, we should not be surprised when our citizens, and notably some of the best educated younger ones, express their convictions violently.

In trying to formulate the goals of higher education for the coming years, we must preserve the best in both of the styles and find ways of arbitrating the differences. The virtue of the analytic style is that it gives the individual precision tools with which to manipulate his environment. From it, we should preserve the degree of objectivity and rational method required to support intercourse among individuals with different aims and talents, and we should retain the principle that knowledge of what happened in the past and in cultures different from ours is essential to our survival and must not be lost. The virtue of the engaged style is that it demands human contact between the individual and the object of his attention; it has shown us that a legitimate function of higher education can be to help people to formulate and actively to observe ethical and aesthetic convictions.

The proposals that follow are calculated to promote a climate in higher education that will be hospitable to the positive aspects of Engagement. The situation of the arts today is too fluid to support programs with fixed concepts of what constitutes the fundamentals of art or its essential techniques and methods. I believe that the curriculum most likely to be effective in the coming years will be one planned for flexibility, the courage to take risks, and the readiness of teachers to learn from the response of students.

THE SEGREGATION OF THE ARTS IN EDUCATION

Education in the age of objective analysis has emphasized the acquisition of verbal and mathematical skills, and has assigned the arts to a peripheral role; like athletics, they are intended to exercise faculties not central to learning.

Americans are ambivalent about the arts; we simultaneously reject and accept them as serious pursuits by assigning them a special but segregated position in our life and education. Not only the society as a whole, but the teachers of art in the schools and their colleagues in the colleges and universities are willing to compromise with an educational system that neither includes nor excludes art.

Arguments against giving the arts a vital role in education may come on the one hand from hard-headed materialists, and on the other from the intellectual elite.

The materialist measures educational value quantitatively, and finds that the art student learns nothing palpable or useful. He sees the activity of making or performing not as a path to knowledge but simply as self-expression; putting-out rather than taking-in.

The intellectual recognizes the seriousness of the arts, but characteristically believes that they should be practiced and studied outside the system of higher education. He perpetuates the aristocratic educational tradition of the Middle Ages and Renaissance, when the visual arts were called "mechanical" (as opposed to "liberal") because artists worked with their hands and got dirty; a gentleman and a scholar might dabble in the mechanical arts or theorize about them, but he would not practice them. Accordingly, the serious art student is directed to a professional art school or conservatory, and the college student is allowed the option of electing a few studio courses primarily on the grounds that they "broaden experience."

We should find it easier to define the function of a visual arts education if we clarified our concept of creativity. No faculty would offer an elementary physics course called "creative science" because the subject is sufficiently respected to make it obvious that creative innovation demands experience and training; yet beginning students are often offered "creative art." We confuse two processes by giving them the same name. In its proper sense, the creative act is the conception of a unique response to nature or existence that offers an illuminating way of perceiving or feeling; in the abused sense, the creative act is simply the process of giving shape to unconscious impulses by forming or expressing something; the fact that this "something" may be a painting rather than a mud pie does not give it superior stature, and does not confer educational value on the experience of making it. Education in art should be thought of as a discipline that helps the student to consciously articulate the form-making impulse without losing the power of its irrational and emotional origins. If we defend the arts in higher education by emphasizing the "creative" impulse rather than the discipline, we imply that their primary role is to provide libidinal release; if that were the case, they could justifiably be kept apart in a class with other recreational activities.

The grounds for the acceptance of the arts into higher education are paradoxically intertwined with the grounds for rejection. Piously sentimental about that aspect of our culture we call Culture (what is shown by museums, played by philharmonic orchestras or opera companies, reviewed in little magazines, etc.), Americans enshrine the arts in a Pantheon—isolated from the "real" world—where they can be at once revered and ignored. Even intellectuals speak vaguely of the humanizing power of art as if it were an optional luxury available to refine the student or to beautify the environment once practical requirements have been met.

The support of art education as an expendable and isolatable luxury commodity promotes segregation as effectively as outspoken opposition.

As the arts are segregated, so are the artists who are teaching art. In all but the most experimental colleges, a majority of academics, and particularly professors of the history of art, music, and literature, would dispense with even the token existing studio and workshop programs. This attitude usually is attributed to the scholar's preference for verbal communication, but since it extends to questioning the value of poets and fiction writers in language departments it evidently is not the absence of words that arouses suspicion so much as the potential presence of unanalyzed feelings. But this Platonic wariness of the disruptive force of art is only one component of the scholar's uneasiness. Another is his impression that college art curricula are insubstantial and undemanding. To the extent that this verdict is well founded, the isolation of the artist-teacher is self-determined and not to be blamed on academic stuffiness. There are powerful *internal* causes for the segregation of the arts.

Advanced teaching in art, as in most other fields today, has focused on problems of technique and form. The discipline is not defined in terms of a content or purpose, but in terms of media and their manipulation.

The control of technique is essential in art, as in any other discipline. But techniques are means that can be selected and developed only in reference to particular ends, and the age of objective analysis has not defined its ends.

The last coherent educational theory in art was that of the Bauhaus, formulated a half century ago; today Bauhaus techniques are taught throughout the world, but their purposes have been forgotten (and, if recalled, they would not seem relevant to today's problems).

Burdened with a curriculum divided by media and level of expertise (elementary and advanced drawing, etching, modeling, and so on), the artist-teacher is given no opportunity or encouragement to redefine his goals. He faces dilemmas—to offer or not to offer life-drawing, and at what "level"—that are insoluble in isolation from the determination of what constitutes the substance or content of his program.

The lack of content in the curriculum makes it impossible for the teacher to learn much in the process of teaching, and makes it difficult for him to bring the most urgent issues he encounters in his own work into the classroom. Whereas a majority of scholars and research scientists benefit in several ways from being teachers, the majority of artists do not; if they teach, it is to make a living and because the teaching is unstimulating it often drags down the level of their own work.

The design of an arts program is complicated by the impossibility of taking refuge in a classical curriculum that ignores the intense controversies of the moment. The alternative is to move with the forefront of the field, like the scientists; but the forefront is hard to identify; the validity of innovation in art cannot be tested empirically. The picture is uniquely distorted by the art world: a complex of artists, critics, collectors, dealers and museums that supplies directly and through the mass media a sequence of fashions at a rapid pace. Should the curriculum keep abreast of this activity by constant shift of direction that would draw the academy dangerously close to the market? Or should it decline to bend with the fashion of the moment and risk obsolescence? The dilemma arises partly from the failure to concentrate on the content of the program; the problem posed by the art world is merely one of form and taste.

An art teacher in our time cannot easily define the content of his discipline. In the Renaissance, art was supposed to communicate certain things, and artists sought the proper form for the communication. Form was a vehicle, in the sense that biography is a vehicle for communicating a certain kind of historical content.

But in modern and contemporary art, form and content are not so easily differentiated; for over a century, problems of form have preoccupied artists until in recent times the content of much of the art has seemed to be the effort to solve formal problems posed by earlier modern artists. I say "has seemed to be" because those who talk and write about abstract art—critics, teachers, even artists themselves—have been forced to over-emphasize form because the content is difficult or impossible to convey in words. Besides, we have been formalists as well as technologists; in much modern art, form is presented as if it *were* content, and much modern criticism and art history is rooted in a method of style analysis dominated by formal criteria.*

What goes on in the college art studio? Students are set to solving problems couched in terms of concepts such as space, surface, structure, color, line, texture. In order to give these abstractions a concrete and teachable character they have to be handled as conventions—a visual counterpart to the categories of grammar. I agree that the grammar must be learned, as technique must be learned, but as a means to some end. An art curriculum that does not pose more substantive problems than those involved in manipulating a language of form has no place in higher education.

Cinema and photography are astonishingly popular among college age students because these arts can be approached easily as mass media without the self-consciousness and exclusivity of "high" art, and because their representational nature makes them accessible to more people with less expenditure of effort. It is increasingly difficult to interest students

---

* My criticism of formalism is not directed against abstract art more than against figurative art; style is irrelevant.

in the problems of contemporary painting and sculpture not, as in the 1950's, because of their resistance to unfamiliar vocabularies, but because the problems that have been occupying artists since that time—such as those of optical or minimal art—do not seem to generate excitement.

The art of our time appears to be radical partly because it has followed the pattern and the strategies of the nineteenth century avant garde. Whether for this reason or another, it has remained immune from the criticism that proponents of the engaged style have leveled against scholarship. But the younger generation is awakening to the fact that the arts have shared increasingly in recent years in the disengagement that characterizes the analytic style. A generation passionately concerned with the social, political and economic problems of our time cannot consistently identify itself with an art, with a critical literature, or with an education in art that is exclusive and turned inward on itself.

These problems can be solved by giving college programs in art the serious substance that they often have lacked in their present isolation and by admitting them to full status and privilege at the core of the curriculum. There are three persuasive arguments for this change:

1. *Training of vision*. The visual arts, like music, offer an effective alternative to the verbal-mathematical modes of expression heavily emphasized in our education system. In the electronic age, when a constantly increasing portion of information is transmitted by means of images, the study and understanding of visual communication is essential. But, as the study of language does not suffice for the understanding of literature, "visual communication" is simply the substratum of a training in art that should reveal the complex relationships of human experience to constructs of visual form.

2. *Physical participation*. In the life class, the darkroom, or the welding studio, students have a chance to learn by making something, by participating physically as well as intellectually in the manipulation of materials to produce the sort of statement that cannot be made in words and figures and that has sensuous dimensions which engage the whole person—body and mind.

3. *Practice as criticism*. The study of the techniques and grammar of art combined with practice and experiment can lead to an understanding of the art of the past and of the present which extends into new dimen-

sions the experience gained in historical and critical discourse. The attempt to solve personally and in a contemporary idiom problems that have challenged artists in the past can give a vivid grasp of their nature.

Whether training in art can be integrated successfully into the liberal arts education remains to be seen. It cannot be systematically programmed in the usual sense because the instructor must be prepared to capitalize on the spontaneous discovery, the irrational insight. In fact, a learning situation will be successful to the degree that it manages to promote the unexpected and afterward to control it.

The character of the academic environment, the tradition of academic tenure, and the goals of the students may tempt instruction to drift toward the intellectual and verbal and away from the visual-sensuous experience. The plan I will propose attempts to meet this problem. It is intended primarily for the academic student rather than for the future artist, so it seeks to bridge the gap between his academic experience and the studio rather than to perpetuate the existing isolation. It involves more discussion and criticism—more use of words, that is—than would be profitable in an art school, in order to make the arts more accessible to the scholar. But it must avoid compromising the unique values of visual experience in the process by overintellectualizing problems and solutions.

A COLLEGE ART PROGRAM

The function of a college art program is to offer general rather than professional education, and to expand the scope of a liberal arts education by offering alternative ways of perceiving and communicating. Its ultimate goal, then, is consonant with that of a liberal arts education.

The goal of education in the age of objective analysis has been to prepare students to analyze objectively. Its limitations as well as its benefits are apparent; the analytic method has shown us how to understand and how to act, but not how to choose what we want to understand and to act upon.

Without sacrificing the technical and operational efficiency of the analytic method, a new goal may be set for college education, of a dual nature directing the internal and external development of the individual.

The internal aspect is the encouragement of *self-realization,* the preamble to effective experiencing and functioning within oneself and within society. The disciplines of art assist this process by giving articulation to the unconscious form-making impulses, subjecting to rational control the forces that well up from the inside and reach for undefined goals. It is the making of civilization reenacted by each individual as he learns to turn a shout of joy into an aria or a mud pie into a figurine. It involves not only the inward search for identity and the drive to express but an accommodation to tradition and to contemporary culture. The more intellectual and scholarly disciplines cannot as effectively help the individual to achieve an integration of the emotional and rational factors in the personality.

The external aspect is ethical: the preparation of the student *to make and to maintain a humane social and physical environment*. This demands a radical change in higher education, because it admits into teaching and scholarship certain judgments of value and actions based upon them.

An ethical aim represents a return to traditions that were abandoned only in this century; before 1900, the purpose of higher education was to prepare a small, privileged group of citizens to assume public responsibility. Today, higher education is more democratic; but the nature of a citizen's responsibility is less well defined, and we do not share religious or philosophical convictions of the kind that made our ancestors sure of the values they wanted to transmit. It is risky to inject ethics into training a large and diversified student population today; but less so than the perpetuation of an education that ignores values.

The program sketched here is organized in three stages. The first would introduce students to *means* of visual expression and communication: techniques and materials, and the principles of composing them into structures. The second stage is a study of *content* and of the bases of judgment of quality and value. The third would *apply the training* either to independent invention or to actual social situations in the environment.

STAGE I

A primary task of the first stage is to counterbalance cultural blocks to perception and visual communication and to restore the natural capacities for making and understanding images that children in our culture display in pre-adolescent years. Adolescents, with the misdirected encouragement of parents, teachers, and the mass media, come to use images simply as re-presentations of facts and events, to lose awareness of their symbolic and expressive character. A picture or sculpture may become for them no more than a substitute for a narrative, and their use in this way reinforces the dominance of the conceptual and verbal over the visual and sensuous categorization of information.

The introduction to techniques and materials should be primarily analytic—the investigation of the components of form and symbolism on which images are made; and because it is analytic, it would not be basically different in approach from the well-conceived introductory courses developed in some institutions in the last generation, or from Paul Klee's *Pedagogical Sketchbook* (a drawing manual), Hans Hofmann's exercises in the relationship of the picture surface to spatial illusion, or Josef Albers' color studies. These should not be presented as academic dogma, as they frequently are, but as frameworks for open investigation. One deficiency of training in the Bauhaus tradition has been the setting of problems that have pre-established solutions or a restricted range of solutions known to the instructor but not to the student, so that investigation becomes a constricted and precise search for the known rather than a penetration into the unknown.

The problem at this point is to avoid focusing on elements of form for their own sake by examining the interaction between form and meaning: Klee's exercises are illuminating because he develops the psychological and symbolic functions of form. The purpose would be not only to examine empirically the operation of spatial effect, color, line, texture, etc., but to study their effect on the viewer, to consider the potentialities of form for conveying feelings and ideas. What does a line of a certain character "say," if anything? Is what it says a quality of the line, or is the viewer conditioned to attribute that quality to it?

The distinction between art and non-art should be avoided in the beginning stage, so that students become aware of the visual environment without the obstacles of pre-established categories, and so that assumptions of what constitutes art may gradually emerge from exchanges in the classroom rather than being either imposed or implicitly accepted. The media of still and cinematic photography are useful because many students tend to be less inhibited at the controls of a machine than facing blank paper or a block of clay, and because readable and discussable images can be produced without extensive practice.

At an early stage of the analysis of techniques and materials—perhaps from the start—students should be encouraged to synthesize the elements into complex structures and to study critically the interaction of technique, form, and symbols. The exercises at this introductory level can develop into compositions, using themes that are as complex as "time" and "probability," or as simple as "crisis," "silence," "rock and roll," so that studies of the relation of form to perception might be tested in the actual making of an image.

The representation of what we see also is necessary to give students training in discriminating and emphasizing elements out of the mass of visual information, and in restructuring the information to communicate a particular response. An unrelieved program of abstract problems neglects the training of the eye and mind, and emphasizes tendencies to turn inward to already acquired resources or habits rather than outward to new experiences.

Works by artists of the immediate or distant past should be examined in relation to problems in the studio, and perhaps analyzed visually in sequences of sketches. At the same time, the implications of differences in the style of individuals, periods or countries might be discussed. The studio program should not be separated from the history of art. Classroom dialogs between the instructor and an art historian can help to illustrate the variety of valid interpretations of the works chosen, and history of art can enter the studio as a stimulus to solving problems raised there.

The first stage might be pursued for two to four semesters, depending on the student's readiness to work at the level of the second stage. Though it may prove to be efficient to offer fundamentals of the basic techniques in a required introductory course, it should not be necessary to fix a sequence of further courses; here, and in subsequent years, students should select in terms of their evaluation of the instructor and of the problems he proposes to set, rather than following an arbitrary pattern of levels on the scale from "elementary" to "advanced."

STAGE II

While the first stage has dealt with the *internal* character and potentialities of the image in itself, the second examines the relationship of works of art to their context of culture and values. Studies of the func-

tion of art in society, the relationship of artistic to scientific, mathematical, political, or other modes of expression serve to place art in a
cultural environment. The study of judgments of quality (comparative
evaluation) and of value (normative evaluation) would not aim to
establish or to follow a particular aesthetic system, but to make apparent
the nature of the grounds on which judgments are made. These two
contextual studies are brought together at this level not primarily
because they are closely related but because they demand of the student
a certain maturity of intellect and sensibility.

This stage clearly involves an integration of the studio program with
work in many other disciplines. It represents a departure in method and
in content from existing studio curricula, and it can be realized only
with the collaboration of teachers who are not artists.

Classroom work would have a specific subject matter rather than
being "advanced painting" or the like. I can suggest a few subjects, but
the actual program offerings must emerge from the interests and specialties of the participating students and faculty. Here are four possible
choices:

Society and Art

An anthropologist presents the art and artifacts of two or three different
cultures, if possible in the original, bringing out the relationship of the
societal structure to the objects it produces; the students question how the
anthropological approach differs from that of the critic and historian of art.
Studio problems might be stimulated by the objects themselves and/or by
the concept of producing artifacts related to the society of our own time.

Aspects of Structure in Nature and Art

A natural scientist offers a series of lectures, demonstrations and small
group discussions on structure from elemental particles to complex minerals;
or a biologist discusses the organization of simple forms of life. Perhaps a
focused comparative study on a theme such as "symmetry" would prove
more effective. Concurrently in the studio, students study the implications of
natural structure for the making of structures in various media.

Visual Perception

A psychologist leads discussions on the nature of perception with emphasis on the way we receive visual information; the way our experience and
expectation affects what we perceive; the artist's perception of his environment; the viewer's perception of a work of art and its implications for
criticism. Studio projects pursue problems of illusion, with emphasis on the
relation of the individual to the visual world around him.

Man and Machine

An instructor with a philosophical or literary background — a poet might be a good choice — examines different modern images (in literature, art, theater, and film) of the theme: *man and the machine*. This could be the introduction of the fundamentals of linguistic analysis and a consideration of its relevance for work in the studio. The theme becomes the stimulus for two sorts of work in the studio: one, a visual essay on the subject of the course, and the other the employment of a machine in the making of an object (for example, the use of computer graphic techniques to produce a print), combined with discussion of the potentialities of the technique as an art form.

Instruction in quality and value should not be put among the electives at this stage, but should either be a required seminar or should enter every part of the second stage in the form of a periodic scheduled discussion. The best subjects for discussion would be original works of art, both of the past and of the present. Colleges that have no access to permanent art collections might acquire small study collections of graphic art at modest cost (particularly work of living artists), and might take advantage of the many circulating exhibitions that are available. Contemporary art has a salutary leveling character, as it removes from both the professor and the student the authority and support of received opinion. Analysis and criticism of critical writings, rather than the literature of aesthetics, would help in mapping the area of study because the method is rather one of generalizing from instances than of abstractly establishing standards. These sessions should again bring together students and faculty in studio and art history courses; they should seek to encourage diversity and tolerate conflicts of opinion rather than to produce unanimity.

STAGE III

At the third stage, I propose to offer students alternative paths based on the two aims I have suggested for higher education.

One path attempts to further the process of self-realization by independent work that at the option of the student would or would not be presented to faculty members for criticism. Because supervision and instruction are desirable for inexperienced students or for those below a certain level of knowledge and experience with the tools and processes of an art, this path presumably could be offered within an honors program.

The other path is the exercise of art in action—the actual practice of communication between the student in art and an audience. At this level, individuals and teams should work with the community inside the college and out, to make visual stimuli in dull environments, temporary constructions in vacant lots, films or slide tapes for use in schools or hospitals, visual presentations for instructors in scientific fields, posters for local lectures and concerts. Only rarely could students engaged in such projects depend on being commissioned by clients eager for their help; they would have to create a demand by exercising their ingenuity and by using the techniques of communication to gain the cooperation of people of various backgrounds. They would themselves take on responsibilities of education, not only of each other, but of the community, particularly of the young, who might be taken on as apprentices; and they would be testing their social and political concepts and influence, in improving the physical environment and in counteracting visual blight. The social emphasis of the second path is consistent with the non-professional direction of the program and would be unsuitable for those planning to continue as artists—though future designers, film makers, architects, and others who serve the public more directly might benefit from it.

The first stage in this program is similar to introductory stages of most existing programs except in the added emphasis on content, and in the more extended and less sequential course organization. It is exclusively concerned with problems that can be solved in a studio context; first, with *visual analysis,* and then with *visual synthesis.* Because it does not require particular maturity of the student, it could be offered at the secondary school level to students at any age above twelve to fourteen. The advantage of initiating a curriculum of this kind at the secondary level is that it offers opportunities for awakening the inventiveness and confidence of many young people who do not express themselves best in verbal and mathematical languages. The students who have educationally weak backgrounds and the growing number who have been raised on television rather than on books are especially in need of this alternative. The irony is that if the program is deferred to college level, those students best equipped to benefit from it may have been eliminated by the verbal bias of the College Board.

The second stage in the program must be offered at the college level because it assumes in the student both the intellectual maturity to find parallels between forms and concepts in art and those in other fields, and the emotional maturity to make judgments of value in relation to his convictions. It also demands of the faculty not only knowledge but the flexibility to see how knowledge acquired through conventional channels is applicable in an unfamiliar context.

The third stage requires the maturity on the one hand to set and to solve one's own problems and on the other to deal with people in practical situations and to listen to them with humility. This experience is appropriately planned for the end of a college career because it constitutes a transition to the next stage in a student's life, when he assumes greater personal responsibility. At this stage, academic values are tested in actual situations with teachers in the role of guides and associates rather than mentors.

IN CONCLUSION

I have identified as the goal of a liberal education the achievement of self-realization and the making of a humane social and physical environment, and suggested a program on that premise. Self-realization is the necessary preamble to effective action in any context; education always has sought to foster it, but in a restricted spectrum of disciplines that has not properly incorporated experience in the arts. A higher education empowered to promote the making of a humane environment assumes a radically new function and sets out in a direction that cannot be precisely defined beforehand.

What one of us calls humane, another may not, particularly when social imperatives seem to clash with aesthetic standards. As an example, really low-cost housing is generally dreary; handsome design or the rehabilitation of interesting old houses is generally expensive. But we are speaking of education in a democratic, pluralistic society; we must live with diversity and tolerate vague goals. If we set more specific goals than I have done, they would not be adopted. If teachers are to discuss quality and value in the classroom, they can say how judgments are made and can encourage students to make them, but they must not say what the judgments should be. Each student has to develop a standard, and we have to assume that it will be roughly consistent with our own and with that of other students. I make this assumption when I suggest training for public action; if the action had no consistency, or if it were contrary to the general interest, it would produce chaos.

The power of tradition to hold a culture together and to sustain ideals and aspirations justifies my confidence. The subconscious transfer of our deepest beliefs from generation to generation guarantees that we can more or less agree on the outlines of the "humane environment." Another tradition, defined by our analytic methods, is represented in the works of our ancestors that we choose to identify as our heritage. This tradition functions like the individual memory, employing selected experiences from the past partly as a guide to coping with the present. We should be lost without it, because it helps us to perform innumerable small tasks and it frees us occasionally for larger ones. Our thoughts about the larger ones are always conditioned by the traditions we choose. So, in setting new educational goals and programs, we inevitably keep the core of what we have inherited and we change less than we keep.

The goal of past education was to instill predetermined values. The goal of present education is to teach method, because the values are unclear. The education of the future must find ways of confronting values without imposing them.

SEVEN

Music
and
Education

NORMAN LLOYD

The special insight that the artist-teacher can bring to the teaching of the arts is illustrated in an earlier chapter by Robert Watts and again in this chapter, "Music and Education" by Norman Lloyd. To a remarkable degree their concerns are the same. Both men are involved with the question of how people learn. Both, along with James Ackerman, deplore the isolation of the arts from the rest of the college curriculum and share the belief that this is due to a lack of understanding of what the arts are about. One difference between music and the visual arts, however, is the fact that there is a large, potentially receptive student body waiting for proper instruction in music. Norman Lloyd believes that this places a special responsibility on faculty and administration to provide the right approach to music. Among his proposals is a strong argument for interrelating the arts by allowing students to mix the media, which is a point also made by Robert Watts.

Norman Lloyd has taught music to liberal arts students at Sarah Lawrence College, to physical education majors at New York University, and to undergraduate and graduate musicians and dancers at the Juilliard School of Music. At Juilliard he and William Schuman established the non-traditional courses in music theory known as the "Literature and Materials of Music." Before joining The Rockefeller Foundation in 1965 as its first Director for Arts, Norman Lloyd was Dean of the Oberlin College Conservatory of Music. His publications include works for piano, chorus, violin and band, and books such as The Golden Encyclopedia of Music, The Fireside Book of Folksongs *(with Margaret Boni), and* The American Heritage Songbook *(with Ruth Lloyd).*

While the world of education is awakening to the fact that radical changes in aims and modes of operation are needed, the world of music has been swept by winds of change that are hurricane-like in their intensity and scope and have serious implications for education. Forces are at work in every sector of musical life, altering and questioning traditions and habits. A musical revolution is taking place—in musical aesthetics, compositional techniques, performance practices, concert-going habits, and educational approaches. But the revolution is one with a positive aim; not to destroy our musical heritage, but to expand it. Instead of being limited in time and geography, musical interest has opened up so that it encompasses the present as well as the past, the non-European as well as the European. There is a breaking down of arbitrary differences that have been built up between so-called "high" and "low," "native" and "exotic" cultures.

Much of the ferment is due to the development of new audiences. Radio and recordings have nurtured this largely young audience. This "second audience" is naïvely sophisticated and almost too permissive. It tolerates practically anything, aurally, but it has the virtue of not ruling out certain sounds or types of musical organization because of a false sense of musical tradition. It throngs to concerts of music by Harry Partch, buys out the hall for an all-Rameau concert, and collects recordings of music by Varèse, Handel, Monteverdi, and the newest "pop" group. It listens to the kind of FM "good music" stations that program within a single hour Hindu ragas and bossa novas, African folk songs, and Gregorian chants, plus a mélange of Bach, Stockhausen, Copland, and Mozart. When it listens to the radio it has a high degree of tolerance, but when it buys tickets it is highly selective and is not interested in buying a subscription series. Whenever possible it wants to listen in informal surroundings and in informal attire.

This audience is truly the audience with the eclectic ear—an audience that has a real hunger for music, a hunger that it satisfies by listening to music on records, tape recorders, radios, and by going to live concerts and performances. Most of the listening habits of this audience have developed in spite of parents and teachers. The real instructors have been the group peers and the disc jockeys, who sell a musical point of view along with their commercial products. In some mysterious way —and often betrayed by its leaders—the young audience has managed to take its many-faceted enthusiasms from a variety of sources, possibly because it does not trust any one source. It is above all an audience that believes in participation. It sings-along, it plays guitars, and it makes up much of its own material.

It is a never-ending source of amazement to me that young people are attracted to music, because in many ways the educators seem to have gone out of their way to make music, and the arts in general, as unpalatable as possible. Music-making is scheduled for after-school hours. Out-of-tune pianos pollute our high school and college auditoriums. The narrow scope of most teaching does not give students the chance to discover the dynamic, changing aspects of music. The masterpieces are forced on them, rather than discovered as great works as they go through life. Instead of music, we teach subjects, such as harmony, counterpoint, analysis, history. Within each of these subjects there is a further emasculation of a great art. Music becomes a series of formulae; history becomes involved with trivia; and the study of musical form and style is limited to a consideration of musical practices bound in time by the eighteenth and nineteenth centuries and in geography to that stretch of music-land that lies between the Rhine and the Danube. The symbols of music are studied—but not sound, not the essence.

In our colleges, the study of music is so recent an addition to the liberal arts curriculum that not too long ago it was common for students to pay extra fees for music lessons because music was something that had little or nothing to do with formal education. There is still some hesitancy on the part of educators to fully accept the study of music as central to the core of humanistic learning, except for those courses where music is verbalized rather than made. This emphasis on talking about music, rather than making it, is not new. Its origin goes back at least to the early sixth century when Boethius, himself a talker rather than a doer, said that the most important thing to do about music is to talk about it, thus assigning the composing and performing of music to secondary importance.

An education that has traditionally been associated with verbalization, as ours has, puts the value of a course in quantitative terms involving verbalization. It is enough to be able to distinguish between the sounds of Bach and those of Stravinsky; to be able to discuss or chart the usual musical forms of the baroque and classical periods; and to have the proper reverence for the acknowledged fifty masterworks.

We have been guilty in fact of both oversimplifying and over-complicating the art. We have taught the history of music as a main-stream that runs directly from Pope Gregory to Bernstein, giving the impression that the course of music ran straight and true, instead of letting our students discover that it meanders like the Mississippi. The importance of some composers and some movements have been over-emphasized, while the contributions of others have been ignored.

At times we have operated like ancient Egyptian priests, making arcane and mysterious that which should have been warm and human.

We have overrated much that was merely pretentious, and underrated that which was simple and honest. We have even tried to convince our students that a dull symphony, because it was a symphony, was of greater value than a beautiful short piano work or a poignant song.

But now the present musical revolution is giving us all a chance to redefine what we believe music is all about. Because of various pressures we need to find out the values in all contemporary musical manifestations—from Cage to the Beatles, Schuman to Ellington, Xenakis to Shankar, and Penderecki to Ray Charles. New electronically-generated sounds have even made us redefine, if possible, the difference between music and noise.

WHAT IS MUSIC, AFTER ALL?

The first thing to know about music is its universality as well as its diversity. Music is the language of the emotions, but it is not *a* language. It is many languages and sub-languages, all starting from the same premise: that musical sounds can be used to communicate ideas and feelings. Music, of all the arts, is the most direct and, at the same time, the most inaccessible. It is as simple as the nonverbal sounds we make when we laugh or cry. It is as complex as a late Beethoven string quartet that exists not only in tone but in highly sophisticated time spans that counterpart one another in a continuum rather than in a simultaneity. Music exists by itself and in many combining forms. Music is a part of religious ritual and ceremonial pomp. It is opera and folk music, symphony and children's singing games, dance music that inspires our muscles, and Bach's "St. Matthew Passion" that stirs our souls. It is tribal chant, the Rotary Club luncheon sing, the group bursting spontaneously into song at a party, the shepherd playing his flute in his loneliness.

Music, because of its possibility of ranging over every aspect of human emotions, can give us a sense of the depth of human anguish as well as a sense of the ultimate ecstasy. It can tell us how great a man's spirit can be and encourage us to develop greatness within ourselves. It is concerned with giving us a vocabulary of feeling.

Man lives in what to him is eternity. He deals with time in the rhythm of nature and makes arbitrary subdivisions of that rhythm. He is, however, unable to comprehend the infinity, the vastness of time. In many ways he is like the swimmer who is aware that he floats in water but is not conscious of the "waterness of water." Music, because it exists in time, treats time as a material substance, stretching through it, decorating it, and existing in it.

Whether as performer or composer, anyone who is involved in music is constantly putting to himself the question, "What will happen if . . .?" As a performer, he tries to play or sing a work in different ways to discover the different meanings that the composer has placed there. He is constantly recreating what the composer sketched out in his symbols for time and pitch. He is, if he is a good performer, always searching for new hidden relationships to be added to his previous knowledge of the composition. He does not play by rote but by searching. The composer is of course totally involved with the creative act.

Music must therefore be thought of as something living, vital, and necessary. It must be accepted for what it is: a way of expressing man's emotions. It is not part of the veneer of gentility but something that lies deep within man himself and can be cultivated only as man himself is cultivated. It is a way of understanding the society of human beings, not as groups of ethnic curiosities but as fellow travelers along life's paths.

The study of music must be taught as a way of gaining insight into the creative process, at the same time giving an awareness of the need for discipline and the use of controls. One thing that is often forgotten, when discussing music, is that it is based on mental and physical techniques. It is not enough to want to play the guitar or the piano; one must practice so that muscles respond almost automatically to what the brain commands. And, conversely, having the fleetest digital technique is of little value if the brain has no concept of what music is all about.

To summarize, for the moment: the study of music should give the student an understanding of the scope of the art. It should give him an insight into the dynamic nature of society, since music is as ever-changing as society itself. The study of music should develop the student's sensibility to aural events, making him aware of sound, noise, and quiet. It should also give the student a sense of the cultural past and present, relating his background to other cultures. It should give the student a feeling of what it means to be a creative person, recognizing that the act of creating is within the reach of everyone. Finally, the study and practice of music should be approached as something that affects the growth of one's emotional powers.

WHAT CAN BE DONE: BY ADMINISTRATORS?

Too often administrators have tended to deprecate the role of the arts in their institutions; they often act as though there is something embarrassing and not quite manly about the arts. This attitude is changing as administrators are beginning to realize that many students *do* take the arts seriously. But the process of change is slow. Much remains to be done about accepting music and the other arts into the center of the curriculum, and ultimately it is the administrators who are responsible for seeing that something is done. Their first priority must be to force a change of educational philosophy relative to the arts. There must be recognition that rehearsing a madrigal can be as intellectually rewarding as dissecting a frog; that learning to read music is as worthwhile as studying a language. If credits are the necessary incentives, then work in music should be equated with work in the other areas of college and university study.

One sore point in student-administration relationships is the lack of scholarship and fellowship aid; students in the arts see their fellow students in the sciences or other traditional disciplines favored, by reason of government and foundation fellowships, and bequests from football-loving alumni. In most cases the school of music within a university is so new that it has not generated endowment funds for student fellowships. To respond to this problem administrators should find ways for students in the arts to be equally eligible for student-aid funds and also encourage prospective donors to earmark funds for the arts.

But more important than the granting of credit and awarding of scholarships is the creation of an atmosphere favorable to music—an atmosphere that encourages the student as composer, performer, and listener. This can be done by providing enough music rooms with pianos so that students can practice individually or gather together in groups to make music informally. While this might seem a minor point, in many schools there is such a tangle of red tape about the use of practice rooms that students are discouraged instead of encouraged to make music. Participation in chamber music, jazz groups, and small choral groups should be made easy. Lounges and living rooms lend themselves to just the right relaxed way in which to play, sing, or just listen. Formal concerts and recitals are important, but not all valuable experiences in music take place under such circumstances.

Another important part of a congenial atmosphere is the availability of records and tapes and the facilities for playing them. Record collections should be comprehensive and include jazz, folk songs, and ethnic records, as well as concert music. Students should be encouraged to browse through these collections, finding new areas of interest as they explore.

As part of the musical atmosphere, colleges and universities should provide opportunities for hearing live concerts, particularly of twentieth century music. Many large universities have resident chamber groups, some composed of faculty members or graduate students, or a mixture of both. It is easier for the large universities such as the University of Michigan and the University of Iowa to support such ensembles, but there is no reason why groups of small colleges can not cooperatively establish their own resident performing groups, sharing services of the group as colleges now share libraries and computer facilities.

Above all, there must be freedom and a hospitable climate within the college for experiments that interrelate the arts. The basically romantic period notion of the merging of the arts, one into the other, has taken the contemporary form known as "mixed media." To properly work in developing new forms, students must be able to move freely from music studio to art studio, from film workshop to dance workshop. As the rigid boundaries in the arts are breaking down so, too, must administrative rigidity give way to administrative flexibility in dealing with the arts.

The adminstrator's lot is not an easy one and in dealing with the arts he not only must be sympathetic but must make every effort to get to know what the arts are all about, since he is the one who must champion the arts and defend them against attacks from outside—and inside—forces that attempt to denigrate the value of the arts in education.

WHAT CAN BE DONE: BY TEACHERS?

But despite any changes in philosophy on the part of administrators, no real change can be effected without the positive support of the faculties. The teachers of music will have to make radical adjustments in the ways they approach their subject. A thoughtful assessment of what should be offered to students is needed in every college. If the aim is to turn out students who can hold their own in cocktail conversations about music, then the present ways of doing things seem adequate. But if this goal is found to be too limited, then courses must be reconstructed so that faculties can strike out boldly from the past methods of teaching to explore new territory and find new paths. Each college situation is unique, as is each class of students, and every faculty must determine its own way of presenting musical truth.

My first concern would be that students learn how to deal with the basic elements of music, experimenting with sounds and the organization of sounds in time. From the very beginning they should be helped to think compositionally, making short phrases that utilize only rhythmic elements, as in a percussion score, or writing melodies that can be sung or played on various instruments. From the very beginning, students should be urged to improvise—at the keyboard, singing, or playing instruments—so that they learn how to speak in terms of music itself. Improvisation is a basic part of compositional practice and every composer mentally improvises as he works. Improvisation, however, must be controlled and disciplined; it is not a form of self-expression.

Parallel to work in the basic techniques of composition, students should investigate a tremendous amount of musical literature, learning how other composers have manipulated sound. As a result of this investigation the students will soon begin to see that the acceptability of certain musical ingredients within a culture varies greatly from one period of time to another. The very fact that we isolate and label style characteristics by period — Renaissance, baroque, etc. — indicates the changes in musical taste and techniques that occurred in Western Europe in the past.

Explorations in musical literature should not be concerned with only the mountain peaks of European music, such as Bach's Passions and Wagner's "Ring." Exploration should be broad enough to include the valleys, the meadows, and gentle hills of the world of music. Teachers should remind their students that "culture" is not just what happens at the Metropolitan Opera House or Symphony Hall. There are values in all kinds of music and students should be encouraged to find the good that exists in a jazz combo, a symphony, or a folk song. The students of course know this already; it would be reassuring, however, to have the teacher share this knowledge.

College classes in music should investigate music of all cultures, not just the music of Western Europe. There is an inherent value in getting to know any art from another culture. But there is the added value that comes when one begins to compare music of several cultures. The student is often able, by making such comparisons, to stand aside and see his own culture for what it is. He learns to appreciate the mighty works that have been composed in Europe in the past, but he also learns that there have been ways of making music in Africa, Asia, as well as the Americas, that are evocative. (Strangely enough, students in the United States often know more about European culture than about their own.)

From the study of the basic elements, as found in music from all times and places, students are then ready to go into details of such traditional subject matter as harmony and counterpoint. They are now able to understand why they are studying such techniques and exactly how important such techniques are in total musical education. Understanding the ever-changing aspects of music leads to an awareness that the creative person is dealing with possibilities, not just probabilities. Students can, by creative teaching, be led to see the function of rules and that rules are based on practices of the past. From this point on the students can easily learn how to make their own textbooks—if they so desire.

Then there are the new sounds, generated electronically, which provide interesting challenges to both the students and the teachers. Some teachers are now teaching basic musical composition by means of taped sounds. By doing away with the problems of music notation and the skills needed in learning how to play an instrument, students using taped sounds are confronted with the basic elements of music itself: sound and time. On the simplest level they can soon learn how to put together a montage of interesting sounds. As they progress they discover the great problems that one faces when one juggles time. Splicing tapes can teach them a great deal about time as they put together long or short segments of tape until a psychologically right balance is struck. Once students are aware of this balance they can begin to understand how Stravinsky or Beethoven, or the Javanese or Indians, dealt with segments of time to create musical form.

The danger in limiting students to taped sounds is the same danger that lies in limiting students only to the harmonic vocabulary of the eighteenth century. Sooner or later students who start with electronic manipulation of sounds must learn how to deal with the more conventional ingredients of music. The combination of composition—improvised, written, or created electronically—and compositional analysis should give students a good start toward understanding the hows and whys of music.

Analysis, however, should not be approached only as a discussion of musical molds (sonata, fugue, etc.), although these large-scale methods of organization need to be learned. The best analysis is that which discusses the inner ingredients of music, such as understanding the function of a chord as Beethoven might have used it or the effect of dropping an odd-numbered meter into a succession of four-count measures. The student should, as he analyzes, savor the delightful things that the composer does as he juggles his sounds, and enjoy them as the composer probably did as he wrote. The more the student can understand the rules of the game—that is, the limitations that a composer has placed on himself—the more he will understand and appreciate skillful work, whether it be symphony, ballad, dance piece, or instrumental tour de force. Such an understanding of a compositional practice equips the student to become what William Schuman has described as the "virtuoso listener." He listens to music as some people watch a game of baseball. He is like the boy who, having grown up playing baseball, football, or basketball, knows the intricacies of the game and, when on the sidelines, watches not only with an eye to what has happened or what is happening but also with the sense of what the various possibilities are in the next play or series of plays. In the ball game, the manager or coach is the creative person who can decide to ignore the expected and aim for the element of surprise. In music, it is this same element of surprise that the good composer can introduce just often enough to keep the listener alert for what might happen next. But one can be surprised only when one understands enough to anticipate what is likely to happen. Knowledge of traditional procedures must go hand in hand with knowledge of the possibilities that exist at every given moment in the life of an art form. Analysis must always be thought of as a means and not an end. The right kind of analysis of music should make better performers as well as better listeners. There is no better way of investigating music than by participating in the making of it, arguing, discussing, and analyzing as one plows through a piece of chamber music, a jazz improvisation, or a madrigal. I believe that it is infinitely better to perform a symphony with whatever and whomever is available within a classroom than to listen passively to a record. The next step, after arriving at an understanding of a work through participation, would be to listen to five or six recorded performances of the same work for the purpose of studying the tremendous variety that exists as performers from various backgrounds look at the same musical work.

THE ARTS SPEAK TO THE BIG QUESTIONS

While ostensibly students should be taught something about music, actually, I would hope they would be learning something about themselves and their world by means of music. From music the student can find out what he is, as a thinking and feeling human being. He can learn how to discipline himself so that he can perform with others. Music training can cultivate the student's aural discrimination, sharpening his sense of hearing so that he hears his environment as well as sees it. In a world gradually becoming polluted by noise as well as by chemicals and refuse it is important to realize that our aural senses are being dulled. Lost to us is the great sensitivity to sound that Thoreau possessed and disclosed in his journals. Contemplating and writing in a quieter culture, he heard symphonies in the humming of the telegraph wires, and cantatas in the chirping of the birds.

The mystery of the lure of music has not been solved by anyone and perhaps at this point it is possible only to ask questions. Why, for example, in this most permissive age, are so many students drawn to the most disciplined of all art forms? Is it because in music one starts with perfection—playing or singing the right note at exactly the right time— and goes on from there? Is it because music, along with the other arts, has been telling us the truth about ourselves and our society, at a time when young people have been disillusioned about those who speak to them in words? Is it because a musical experience is a very personal one, in an age when everything is becoming de-personalized? Or is it because music provides a common experience as well as an individual one, bringing us together in a world of brotherhood and peace?

The real meaning of all this may be that the arts are the true humanistic studies of the contemporary world. In their direct way they are speaking to the big questions: Who are we? and where are we going?

EIGHT

Notes on a Visit to a Distant Campus

PETER CAWS

The scheme sketched in the following chapter should be taken as a general proposal for the reform of higher education, adapted to the subject of this book. Peter Caws explains the form in which he has couched the ideas:

"The scheme is utopian, but it could have been written in a less obviously fantastic mode. Three things account for the departure from the conventional: first, all my earlier attempts to write about this subject

straightforwardly resulted in turgid prose of the kind generally associated with committee reports; second, thinking about the subject in the summer of 1968 persuaded me that the prospects for short-term change of any significant kind were extremely gloomy, the necessity for long-term change of a totally radical kind absolutely imperative; third, finding in the apartment in Paris where we were staying a copy of William Morris's News From Nowhere *infected my language as well as my thought."*

Since he came to this country from England sixteen years ago, Peter Caws has been involved, one way or another, in higher education—as a student and professor of philosophy, and for an interval as an officer of Carnegie Corporation.

He is currently a professor of philosophy in Hunter College of the City University of New York, and directs the university's Ph.D. program in philosophy. Trained as a physicist as well as a philosopher of science, he has been concerned among other things with the relations between various compartments of the intellectual and moral life. One of his books, Science and the Theory of Value *(Random House, 1967), explores certain parallels between science, morality, and art, finding in art the paradigm of value in a free society.*

At breakfast the Dean asked if there was any aspect of the work of the University that I would like to see first, and remembering a former preoccupation I suggested that we might begin with the place of art in the curriculum. He winced a little at the word "curriculum" and, while we walked over a system of elevated paths to a building in a neighboring part of the city, reminded me of our conversation of the previous evening. "The idea of a course of study, as you used to call it," he said, "seems to us unnecessarily narrow. As an image of educational progress at a time when movement from one place to another was restricted to two dimensions, when there were race-courses and railroads and the dominant attitude to life was commercial and competitive, it is understandable enough, but that it should have lasted even into your own time really seems extraordinary.

"Now of course we realize that education is one of the processes whose best model is the brain rather than the machine. It must surely have been known to your contemporaries that the paths followed by energetic discharges in the brain are multiple and variable, and that if a connection isn't made one way it can be made in many others. The idea that in order to become educated a man must follow a single or even a definite path is quite out of keeping with the nature of the enterprise. To begin with, one can't have the slightest idea in advance what the person in question will want to do, so that all specificity in educational goals is automatically repressive. Just as the eye, the hand and the brain are perfectly general instruments—the eye sees everything presented to it, not just (say) works of art, even though it was a well-known aberration in former times to train some eyes to see only works of art; the hand can manipulate anything it encounters, not just buttons and levers; the brain can turn its attention to any problem, not just scholarly ones—so the ensemble of skills and knowledge derived from education must put the individual in a position to do or to know anything whatever, not just foreign languages or literary criticism or physics or philosophy. What you used to call specialists we would be inclined to call freaks, since with the development of their special skills often went an almost total atrophy of the normal ability to do other things."

"I don't see how," I said, "unless there really has been an evolution of the brain, you can have people operating on what we used to call the specialist level in more than one or two fields at once, particularly if the fields have grown since my time in the way one would normally expect. As I remember we used rather to lament the necessity of specialization, but it was forced on us by what was called the 'knowledge explosion.' People simply couldn't keep up, even with other workers in neighboring disciplines, even sometimes with their colleagues in different branches of the same one. Of course you must have very advanced computers to keep track of purely factual matters. The accumulation of facts, the sheer size of the disciplines, was beginning to overwhelm us, so that it was as much as one man could do to become master of his own sub-discipline."

"We do have computers, of course," replied the Dean, "but you're right in perceiving that that is not really the important point. As far as that goes, *you* had books, and if you had made better use of them what you call the knowledge explosion would not have seemed nearly so formidable. Your system of examinations, as I understand it, was a survival from a time when there were no books, or very few, so that it was important for a man to be able to carry a great deal of knowledge in his own head. To give an examination in a subject where standard reference books exist, and yet to deny access to those books for the purposes of the examination, seems to us the greatest conceivable absurdity. What you want to know is whether a man can handle a given problem with the resources at his disposal, and in the academic world—indeed in most parts of the world at large—books were already by the eighteenth century the standard resource for the solution of most problems, both practical and intellectual. To make a virtue of knowing precisely what you don't need to know, at least not in that form, is just perverse.

"But the books (or computers) which contain the facts are only a small part of the story. There are and always have been books which deal with methods of handling the facts; the methods become as it were second-order facts, and then, if you can read the book, you don't need to know the method—at least you don't need to know it in all its details, although of course you need some degree of practical acquaintance with it. And this process repeats itself at even higher levels. The one thing we have learned is that it is more important to have a grasp of the variety of methods, together with practice in a few of them, than to be able to produce at will any number of facts. Language itself is another of the very general instruments I was talking about just now, and we attach much more importance to *complete* mastery of that, than to any one of the specialized things a student might wish to do with specialized parts of it. But you wanted to find out about art, and this will be the best place to begin."

We had arrived, without obviously passing through any doorway, inside a large building, and were beginning to ascend a wide circular ramp, on both sides of which were what looked like spacious offices. The walls of the offices which separated them from the ramp itself were completely of glass, but most of them had curtains pulled across them so that the inside could not be seen. As we passed one of the few whose curtains were pulled back I saw a man in shirt sleeves, sitting at a desk and consulting a large and traditional-looking book.

"Who's he?" I asked.

"That office belongs to Technical Disciplines," said the Dean, "and he is a rather well known practicing attorney; he specializes in international lunar property law. The fact that his curtain is drawn back means that any student can go in and ask him what he's doing. He's a practitioner."

"I suppose he has an office in the city also," I said.

The Dean looked slightly puzzled. "I suppose you could say that that *is* his office in the city," he said. "At least, it's his office, and it's in the city. His firm has a set of offices in one of the commercial buildings, and of course he has full communication with it. But he chooses to work here, because he likes the association with the University, and he does so with the agreement that for a certain amount of time each week—he can set it pretty much as he chooses—he will leave the curtains drawn back. The times will be posted on his door. This building is full of practitioners; the artists are at the top, but I thought you might find it amusing to walk up the ramp rather than going directly—we may catch sight of some other types as we go by."

"He couldn't really be said to teach, though," I said.

"He does as much as anybody does," said the Dean. "As I mentioned to you last night, there are four kinds of staff members on the academic side: instructors, scholars, practitioners, and consultants. Instructors, at the University level, play a comparatively modest role except in some fairly advanced branches of mathematics, although we have a few instructors of reading and writing for students who enter without those skills, and—"

"Good heavens!" I said. "You mean you admit illiterates?"

" 'Good heavens!' sounds quaint," said the Dean. "Like 'zounds' or 'gadzooks'! Illiterates?—everybody can talk, if that's what you mean. But in the etymological sense, yes, I suppose you could say we admit illiterates. It's quite rare for such students to be interested in applying, but we get them occasionally, and the proportion of really brilliant graduates among them is unusually high. Having succeeded in getting that far without reading and writing is, when you think of it, something of an accomplishment in a fairly complex society, and requires verbal and linguistic acumen of a high order. Writing and reading—like computers—are a kind of crutch, really, and when they were invented a quite valuable element of adversity in the environment, which had kept the mind in good intellectual shape, was lost, so that mental standards began to slide. Something similar happened to the body, I dare say,

when automobiles and elevators came along. The educational system of
the schools doesn't compel children to read and write if they don't want
to; most of them do, of course, quite early, but a few hold out, and
often it transpires that they are developing other sensibilities that might
very well have been suppressed by being compelled to pay attention to
books. Even they will know enough to recognize some names and other
basic signs—it's just that they don't depend on the written word for the
communication of everyday information, and with film, television, tele-
phones, voice-sensitive machines, and so on they don't really need to
and we don't keep up the pretense that they do. Your people made a
great mistake, I think, insisting on that kind of literacy for its own sake
even after the basic need for it had been removed.

"*Graduating* without being able to read and write is almost unknown,
though, and the only two cases I'm acquainted with were without doubt
the greatest geniuses I ever met. One made films, and the other was a
poet. He used to *say* his stuff—it was incredible. He got the Nobel
prize for literature when he was twenty-five. I suppose we have less awe
of the written word than your people had—it must have been a com-
monplace of linguistics by the 1930's that the really important thing
about language was its spoken rather than its written aspect. And we
depend on speech more than they did, or at least more explicitly—
although I have seen studies on the communication patterns of your
so-called specialists, and it turns out that the higher up the professional
scale a man was, the less he depended on books and journals and the
more likely he was to call up the appropriate colleague to find out what
he needed to know. In those days it was only when he got that far up
that he knew who the appropriate colleague was, or had the social
standing to approach him.

"We have generalized that system somewhat, so that—as you will see
—there are people whose job it is to steer inquiries in the appropriate
direction. Often that does lead to a book, of course, or a journal or an
encyclopedia. But you'd be surprised how often it happens that some
local scholar has the necessary information, and how delighted he
usually is to have the chance to explain it to someone interested enough
to ask. Scholars don't usually instruct, after all, or lecture very often,
and not having to parade their knowledge for people who almost certainly aren't interested makes it doubly pleasant to do so for those who
clearly are."

We had all this time been ascending, and had now reached what was obviously the top level of the ramp. It had a translucent roof, and the spaces on either side of the corridor, which on the lower level had been offices, were all work spaces or studios of one kind or another. There were no curtains of the opaque sort we had seen below, but instead a system of louvers, also translucent, so that the whole level was permeated with light of an extremely constant and pure quality. There appeared to be very little activity in the studios, and the Dean suggested that we sit down in a kind of lounge in which the long ramp we had been climbing finally terminated.

"Our art people sometimes tend to get started rather late," he said. "I gather they had some kind of celebration last night. So I may as well fill you in on the other duties of the staff. The practitioners you know about, and of course as is only natural there are very many of them in art—that is, people who practice all kinds of arts have their studios and other working space here (they compete for the privilege, in fact) and students come by just to watch them at work and ask questions. Most of the art people are practitioners and nothing else. In other fields, on the other hand, a man may very well be a practitioner and also a consultant; for example, the lawyer you saw downstairs is one. A consultant is just that: somebody whom the student consults when he wishes to make a decision about what to do, or what to do next. On entry to the University every student is assigned to a consultant, and is expected to see him at least once, if only to exchange sociable talk. He isn't obliged to consult the person to whom he is assigned—he may very well know quite well what he wants to do. But he has that resource if he needs it. Of course if all he wants to know is who does what, he can go to one of the information terminals of the University computer system and ask; if there are a number of things he wants to do on the same day, involving his going to a number of different places, and fitting in times when given people will be doing particular things, he will ask the computer to arrange a schedule for him.

"Up-to-date information about what is actually going on is of course one of the central conditions for the day-to-day operation of a place like this. As I understand it, you had access to that kind of information only through periodical catalog publications, newsletters, bulletin boards and other such primitive devices. It often happened that people didn't know what their colleagues were working on, when they would be on hand, what might be a convenient time for a meeting, and so on. Secretaries used to waste hours making telephone calls to people to try to get them together. Now it is a matter of routine for everybody to telephone in to the central data office in the morning with minor changes in the schedule he has submitted for the month. Some people feared, when this system went into operation, that the central administration of the University would always be asking the computer what staff members were doing, so as to check up on them, but I suppose this was a sort of hangover from nineteenth and early twentieth century labor-management problems. In fact, as a safeguard, it was arranged that the computer wouldn't hold anything in its memory more than twenty-four hours after the event to which it referred, and would only respond to specific questions, as to whether, for example, Jones would be available at four o'clock on Tuesday, and not to blanket inquiries as to what Jones was doing with his time. But since most of what people do, apart from their own research, consists in responding to what other people want, rather than in carrying out some routine responsibility, it very quickly becomes apparent if somebody isn't pulling his weight.

"At any rate, the computer takes charge of virtually all practical details like scheduling, making appointments, and such things. It also carries, to the extent that a staff member wants it to, summary details of his current work and things he's interested in, so as to be sure he gets information about what is going on in other parts of the University, can be called on for advice, and so on. Anybody, including students, can request an appointment at one of the terminals, and it will be confirmed provided the man in question hasn't blocked that time, which of course he is perfectly free to do—and so consulting tends to be on a level of intellectual substance rather than, as in your system, making sure that people fulfill certain requirements, make the right connections, and so on.

"As for fulfilling requirements, the central data bank has all that kind of information—what the student is supposed to do, given the category he's in, as well as what he has done—so anybody who is in doubt about his status just goes to the nearest terminal and asks. The consultant serves as a repository of fairly high level information, about the interrelation between fields, for example, or about possibilities for inquiry and learning which haven't even entered the student's head. He doesn't advise or counsel or anything as patronizing as that; he's just available.

But to qualify for the position, he has to have a kind of balanced over-view of the entire enterprise of the University, and that's why rather few artists tend to seek such positions—not that they wouldn't be perfectly qualified if they did, but they are mostly enthusiastically busy with their own things.

"There are a few people who are just consultants; they are the ones to whom most of the entering students are assigned, since they have made it as it were their business to keep up with what is going on everywhere. They can't qualify as full-time consultants, though, unless they have first been either practitioners or scholars. The other group of double appointments tend to be scholar-consultants, although of course we have full-time scholars too. In a way a scholar is automatically a practitioner also, except that what he practices isn't a technical disci-pline which has an independent existence outside the University; he is the person whom historically the University was designed to house and protect, and he is still its most basic reason for being. He does the pure research—advances the frontiers of knowledge, and all that. If he also has the title of practitioner he is, like all practitioners, obliged to set times when students can come to watch him at work and ask questions, and while it might seem at first that that would be a fairly dull occupa-tion, given the traditional image of scholarship, as a matter of fact it often turns out to be extremely profitable. There isn't much to *watch,* it's true, except the scratching of the head, the consultation of texts and references, and so on, but during practice periods (as we call them) a scholar-practitioner can expect to be grilled as to what problem he is trying to solve, why it is important or relevant, etc. As a kind of *quid pro quo* he is entitled to call on any student present to look something up or give a comment or suggestion, which he expects to be intelligent and to the point. Some scholars just aren't temperamentally equipped for this kind of thing, and in that case they won't offer themselves as practitioners. All scholars take specialist students who have arrived at a suitable point in their studies, and direct *their* work, and most of them give occasional courses of lectures, which are announced and which are generally quite well attended, although no formal credit is given for doing so. But then our notion of formal credit must seem rather bizarre to you—"

At this point several students wandered up; they were coming, I gathered, to attend the practice period of one of the University's best-known sculptors. The Dean introduced me as a visitor from out of town (how far out, he did not specify) and suggested that I might like to ask some questions directly of them. I cast around for a suitable topic, and came up with the old question of interdisciplinary work between the arts and sciences. One student responded enthusiastically to this, and proved himself very knowledgeable about the most recent developments in the theory of physical structures, which I gathered were even more highly mathematical than they had been when I was studying the subject. What struck me most, however, was the way in which the student, after making some excellent points about form in science and in art, in particular referring to something called "topological sculpture," ended the conversation. "I'm sorry I can't tell you more about recent developments in physics," he said, "but I signed an affidavit on that some time ago." Here the sculptor evidently arrived at the studio a little way down the corridor, and the students got up and left. The Dean signaled to me to follow, but I held him back.

"Just a minute," I said. "What does he mean, he signed an affidavit?"

"Oh, that," said the Dean. "What he means is that he decided not to continue in physics. When a student stops studying a subject, he signs an affidavit saying that he has been adequately exposed to it, enough at least to make the judgment that he does not want to pursue it further. Before he leaves the University, each student has to file an affidavit for every subject in the catalog except the ones he wants listed on his diploma. This requirement might be viewed, I suppose, as the descendant of what in your day used to be called 'distribution requirements.' Then, I gather, students had to take a number of courses in various disciplines, designed very often for people who were going further in them; and even if a particular student was totally unfitted by temperament and interest for a so-called required subject, he was forced to go through this performance, possibly receiving an extremely low mark. This is another of your practices for which we can see no conceivable justification: pedagogically it seems pointless, psychologically downright malicious.

"Our scheme is in a way the inverse of that. What you were forced to do was to identify some subjects as more important than others, since all could not be required; this insured that the student got only a fragmentary acquaintance with the range of disciplines, and the way in which the introductory required courses were often taught insured maximum irrelevance of these required subjects to each other and to everything else. We on the other hand start with the premise that everything is important, but we don't make the mistake of supposing that because of that, the student should know a bit of everything. What we want him to understand is why various things are important, and in what ways; if we can get that into his head, then he can make a rational choice among subjects when it comes to settling on the line of his own work. If in talking with a consultant the entering student can make a persuasive case to the effect that he knows the structure of a whole area—say the social sciences—but has decided to concentrate in art, he may sign his affidavit in the social sciences at once. Very often the consultant will suggest, all the same, that he take one of the lecture courses in the organization of knowledge, or the interrelation of the disciplines, or something like that, but, depending on how intelligent the student is, even that may not be necessary. On the other hand it is not unusual to find people like the student to whom you were just speaking signing affidavits in individual subjects. That boy, I happen to know, never took a course in physics as such, although he did read for a while with a scholar in the history of science."

"He seems to know a good deal about it all the same," I said.

"Of course," said the Dean, "he's obliged to in order to be able to satisfy the terms of the affidavit. But you see he knows about it in context, not in isolation. We won't let a student abandon a subject until he knows what he's doing, and in finding out what abandoning it really amounts to he picks up more than many students used to when they took the introductory course that stayed within the boundaries of the subject."

"Do people frequently sign affidavits in art?" I asked.

"That's a funny question," said the Dean. "I don't understand the force of 'frequently.' I mean, a good many people list art on their diplomas, which means they haven't signed an affidavit, and the rest of them naturally do sign one. I'll admit that an entering student seldom signs a blanket affidavit in the creative disciplines, because they are so different from one another and because a necessary element of practice, which the student may not have had before, enters even into the degree of acquaintance required in order to satisfy the terms I spoke of. A student who knows enough about the plastic arts will very likely not know enough about music, and so on."

"What about the humanities?" I asked.

"I don't understand you," said the Dean. "What are the humanities?"

This was a question, I recalled, that a good many of my contemporaries had been asking. "Well, it's not exactly easy to say," I said. "You referred just now to the social sciences, and we used generally to divide the work of the University into three broad areas—the natural sciences, the social sciences and the humanities. So the humanities used to include things like literature and philosophy, and sometimes history as well."

"We have five divisions," said the Dean, "and the sciences come out in the same way, but where you had what you call the humanities we have the critical disciplines and the creative disciplines. The difference between a science and a discipline is fairly obvious—in a science the ultimate object is knowledge, about the world or about society, and what practice there is follows from the knowledge, whereas in a discipline the object is an activity, carried out, of course, in a suitably disciplined way. Literary criticism, comparative literature, and most of philosophy count as critical disciplines, whereas the practice of literature goes along with art, music, and the rest into the creative disciplines. The frequency of blanket affidavits runs on a decreasing scale from the social sciences, through the natural sciences and critical disciplines, to the creative disciplines. The fifth division is that of the technical disciplines, which corresponds pretty much to what you used to call the professional schools, but undergraduate students aren't expected to sign affidavits in those. Graduate students are, but that's another story."

We joined the students in the sculptor's studio for a while, but although—as always—the sight of a professional artist at work was absorbing and exciting, nothing was obviously different in kind from studio work in the 1960's. The material in which the sculptor was working was quite unknown to me, and what he was constructing was virtually unintelligible, as I suppose Pol Bury, for example, would have been unintelligible to a mid-nineteenth-century layman. But for these changes I was prepared, and the atmosphere of work, the evident intractability of the material, the sense of a difficult technical problem in the process of solution—all this was familiar. I motioned to the Dean that I would rather talk, and we left the studio together.

"Those students are obviously fairly advanced," I said, "and they are obviously privileged, and know it, to have access to an artist of that caliber. But what really interests me is how art enters into the life of the average student, who isn't going to become a practicing artist. Just watching a great sculptor might of course be exciting even for him, but it doesn't strike me as the most intelligent way to provide an experience of art for the general run of undergraduates."

"What you're really asking," said the Dean, "is what are the conditions for signing an affidavit in art—what, in other words, we consider an acceptable minimum understanding of what art is and how it fits into the pattern of activity in our civilization. I think I could best explain that to you by going back to what I was saying earlier about second-order facts. When our Board of Standards sets the conditions for an affidavit, it generally considers possible knowledge of the subject in question under three headings: direct, indirect, and paradigmatic.

"By direct knowledge we mean the possession of facts or principles in such a way that the student can not only state them on demand but can also give a reasonable account of the grounds of his confidence in them—without which, after all, nothing can really count as knowledge at all. One of the greatest weaknesses of your system was a tendency to give people credit for being able to state—or, what was worse, merely to recognize—factually true propositions, without having the slightest idea of how they would defend the claim to truth if the propositions were challenged. In most areas the affidavit requires that a rather small number of rather central facts be known directly; in some areas none at all beyond the kind of thing to which the science or discipline in question is applicable. The point after all is not to make the student carry around a lot of bits of information, but only to be sure that he knows what's going on.

"Indirect knowledge, on the other hand, is the possession not of the facts or principles themselves but of the means to acquire them; this involves either knowing the methods by which knowledge of this kind can be directly acquired *or* knowing about the literature of the subject, and enough of its language to make the literature accessible with a bit of work.

"Paradigmatic knowledge means having had the experience of solving a problem in the area in question.

"In the creative disciplines direct knowledge is minimal, and so for that matter is indirect knowledge. The history of art and of music, musicology and the rest obviously belong among the critical disciplines, so that apart from technical things—the difference between etching and drypoint, and so on—there isn't that much to know discursively in the arts as such. So in these areas we are forced to rely heavily on paradigmatic knowledge, and that of course is as it should be, since everything in art really hinges on the experience of it."

"I would have thought there was a difference, though," I said, "between actually solving problems in art and for example coming to have an appreciation of it, which might involve direct or indirect knowledge —periods, styles, and all that."

"I think you're mixing the critical with the creative," said the Dean. "The student will have to sign an affidavit in art criticism too—that is, he'll have to know at least how to go about finding and assessing opinions about art, and he will have to have looked at some works. Nobody will try to teach him to *appreciate* them—we will be content if he has really *looked* at them. Of course we shan't leave the looking entirely to chance; there are certain special exhibitions, slide sequences, and the like which exist for people unacquainted with a given period, say, or a given art-form. The principle of organization of these sequences is that becoming acquainted with an unfamiliar form of art proceeds by stages, and that there's no point in plunging somebody into a novel art experience until he's passed through the intermediate stages. To take an example from your own culture, somebody brought up on nineteenth century French classicism (Ingres, for example) would have been totally bewildered if suddenly confronted by a hard-edge work on a shaped canvas (Frank Stella, for example). But if you took him on a visual journey linking the one to the other—through impressionism, cubism, expressionism, pop and op—he might very well follow, and see what was going on, without the necessity of a verbal commentary, which would probably be misleading anyway and would need to operate on too many levels at once to make it at all easy to comprehend, whereas the paintings themselves are directly comprehensible in the context of those immediately preceding.

"But I was going to tell you about the creative side. The basic thing we look for is an awareness that what people do makes a difference to the world—to the way it looks, or sounds, and so on. Most students will be aware, from their earlier studies, either in art history and criticism or (for example) in urban history, or social psychology even, that the way the world looks makes a difference to people, and the complement to that is a realization of how it got that way, namely by conscious (or more often unconscious) design, if I may so put it. I mean, it has hardly ever been man's *intention* to make his environment ugly, but the ugliness that used to be so common—in your cities, for example—was in fact a necessary consequence of the way actions had deliberately been taken for other ends.

"A merely intellectual awareness won't do, however. The student must have the experience of trying to make things look a certain way and finding how difficult that is, and of observing how projects of his own, conceived for other purposes, might have aesthetic consequences of one sort or another. It isn't after all only action that can be creative —there is such a thing as creative perception. So it's a question of training the eye or ear to make rather complex discriminations as a basis for practical aesthetic judgment—not in order to learn conventional standards of beauty or harmony, but to *see* or to *hear* what's actually there, to develop a kind of sensitivity to the visual or auditory environment, and to react to it constructively. The long-term effect of this kind of training, which has become almost universal—it begins quite early in the schools—has been to make the world a lot more pleasant to live in, because once a whole generation arose which not only judged ugliness adversely but was positively *hurt* by it, which couldn't tolerate the billboards and the sirens and the dirt and the fifth-rate architecture, things really began to change. I won't pretend, of course, that we're just a bunch of aesthetes, and plenty of people simply aren't reached by these concerns. But enough are to constitute a powerful social force.

"One of the consequences of this general sensitivity is of course a demand for a great deal of art of the specialized sort. If it's important that the everyday environment be aesthetically satisfying, that argues a level of taste that isn't always going to be satisfied by the everyday environment alone—it will need more intense and more sophisticated experiences from time to time. Really good art is *concentrated* in just this way; one couldn't possibly take it all the time, but it's an indispensable component of experience once one has reached a certain level of awareness. And the demand for it is in exact proportion to the number of people in the society who have reached this level. You must have been aware of an upward trend in this demand, when figures for museum and concert attendance, the purchases of records and art books, and so on, started to rise in a spectacular way.

"The rising level of awareness was quite obviously linked to technical mastery of the reproduction of light and sound, in photography and film on the one hand and radio and recordings on the other. Our social historians tell us that a lot of junk got reproduced at first, but that gradually the aesthetic standards even of popular music and illustration rose, and with them the popular demand for good art. Curiously enough, sensitivity to the everyday environment followed later. The delay was probably due to a combination of reasons—partly because of an atavistic belief that ugliness was a natural concomitant of progress and that beauty in the environment was economically unsound, together with a sort of superstition about the dominance of economic over other values; and partly because people had become accustomed to looking at and listening to the world in very selective ways, so that once outside the museum, for example, they simply didn't use their eyes in the way they used them inside. It was as if awareness and feeling had to be reserved for a few special occasions, and the rest of life spent in a kind of defensive indifference. This seems to us not only sad but also psychologically disturbed. One would have thought that to emerge from a museum into a slum, for example, would have been an unbearable transition, one that would cry out for the transformation of the slum. And in fact the change may have begun when some of your more imaginative people started putting museums in slums.

"But let me get back to the lesson for art education. It lay, of course, in an understanding of the difference that technological advances make to the accessibility of art. I spoke just now about the training of the eye and ear. One of the most disastrous confusions of art education in its early stages was the confusion of that kind of training with the training of the *hand*. People who couldn't make a brush or pencil do what they wanted it to, who couldn't contort their fingers in the appropriate way for a given musical instrument, often became discouraged and even hostile, because it was believed in some circles that that sort of thing was a necessary preliminary to any genuine understanding of the problems of the art in question. There was of course an element of truth in this belief, as was evidenced by the failure of programs of mere appreciation to have any profound or lasting effect on those who were subjected to them. What was needed was clearly some way of sidestepping the merely technical difficulties that lay in the way of practical involvement in art, and giving people of ordinary dexterity a paradigmatic experience of solving an aesthetic problem in some medium or other."

Since leaving the studio we had been walking steadily, part way down the ramp, across a long narrow bridge, through a series of roof gardens and into another building where there was a good deal of traffic and things seemed much more animated than in the practitioners' quarters. I had decided that it was best just to let my host talk, since he seemed to enjoy it so much and since I knew that any question I might ask about the style and plan of the buildings would lead to another long digression. The campus (if it could be called that) was rather like a three-dimensional fantasy by Gaudi, compact but endlessly variable, and on such a scale that every locality seemed small and every vista monumental. It was impossible to tell how far up we were; no drop was more than a couple of stories, but there were wide canyons with steep sides between blocks of buildings, with outside walkways on the setbacks, so oriented as to take advantage of the sunlight. As we entered the new building (again without passing through a doorway, but rather under a high overhang) the Dean digressed in his monolog to tell me about it.

"Nearly all the people you see here," he said, "will be students. Staff members come through occasionally, and some of them are on hand, but the activities that go on in this building, while almost wholly academic, aren't under any direct academic supervision. This is where most of the real work goes on. The reference library is here, there are several hundred computer terminals, there are even more record-reading machines, both aural and visual, there are common rooms and student offices and discussion rooms and so on. We're going to one of the studios where non-professional work in the visual arts is done. The solution to the problem I was just posing, about methods of bringing people to grips with aesthetic problems without putting up obstacles by way of five-finger exercises or practicing color washes, was already obvious to some of your people—we've just generalized it. The simplest and most direct, though perhaps not quite the best, method is to give the student a camera with automatically controlled exposure and send him off to take pictures. As you'll see, the studio is also a gallery, so that he has plenty of examples of good work to compare his own with. On that level—as opposed to the amateur shots he's undoubtedly made before, on vacations, for example—he finds that a technically simple activity like making photographs isn't aesthetically simple at all. An affidavit exercise in the visual arts might consist, say, of one of the student's relatively most successful photographs, along with one of his relatively least successful ones, accompanied by an account, either written or oral, of why he thinks they are respectively among his best and worst. This is pretty routine stuff, though, and the students know it. Most of them try for something more imaginative than that."

The studio turned out to be a whole set of interconnected workrooms, full of students intent on various sorts of activity and construction. They worked with comparatively simple materials: electric light fixtures of various kinds, some familiar and some unfamiliar; projectors, reflectors, and other apparatus associated with what used to be called kinetic art; straight movie equipment and simple apparatus for animation; a good deal of plain material—wood, plastic, metal, etc.—in which assemblages and collages were taking shape; well-equipped drafting tables, and materials for making architectural models; even some conventional charcoal and paper, canvas and oils. "We realize, of course, the Dean was saying, "that the creative really can't be separated from the critical, that just *making* things isn't the whole story. Any creative achievement consists first in making something that didn't previously exist (sometimes in finding something that hadn't previously been noticed), and second in recognizing that it's worth preserving, worth contemplating, worth having attention drawn to it. Then there's the further problem of justifying that recognition. Of course there are lots of stories of people who were 'ahead of their time' in art, who were isolated from their fellows but went doggedly on, warmed only by the inward flame, and all that; but that was a lot easier in a genuinely philistine environment. Here the student is surrounded by people who are really aware of the possibilities of novelty, and you can be pretty sure that if they think something is junk, it is. As a matter of fact, it's quite common for a student to fall back on camera exercises after having tried something more ambitious, like an assemblage, only to find that whatever he did it was still junk. Then when he goes over to the museum of art and sees what a real artist has been able to do with the same medium, he appreciates the achievement as he never could if he came across it without that preparation.

"What this arrangement does, then, is to give students a taste of the creative process with a minimum of preliminary discipline, cutting down the time it takes to arrive at a finished product and bringing the creative-critical judgment (if I can call it that) to bear at the earliest possible moment. It goes without saying that the judgment is generally adverse. Most of what is made here is destroyed almost immediately by the student, and for that reason all the supplies and equipment were at first thought extravagant, and criticized as playthings for grown children, a sort of college-level finger painting. But you have to remember that it really is a serious part of the educational process, and that it exists primarily for the purpose of preparing students for their affidavits. Not all of them sign, of course. Every now and then a natural but unsuspected talent turns up, and in such cases the student will often want the discipline he doesn't get here and will go over to the art people to get it. Most students who go into art seriously go straight into it, though, and don't come here at all."

"What really stays with the ones who sign their affidavits?" I queried. "I mean, it's all very well to spend a few hours a day in a studio for a few weeks, in order to determine that one doesn't want to spend one's whole life there—but beyond that I don't see the positive content of the program, or how it can really have the effect of making people socially conscious critics of architecture, and all that."

"For one thing, it isn't a program," said the Dean. "That was another of your favorite words, I know, like 'curriculum,' and it should have been suspect for the same reasons. A program is what you write down before the event, as with machines, and we do as little of that as possible. The whole point of the affidavit system is *not* to prescribe the form in which a man possesses his knowledge (or lacks it, which from the point of view of his own understanding of himself is just as important). What we know about its success comes from observation of its consequences. One of the things about your methods which is hardest for us to understand is that with all your talk of curricula and programs you hardly ever looked to see what the large-scale results were, so that it wasn't until your society had practically disintegrated that you reluctantly concluded there was a flaw in the educational system.

"The practical result of our non-professional art education happens to be some understanding of and a great deal of respect for the enterprise of art, and a realization that complex objects don't come by aesthetic qualities casually. As to architectural criticism, the analogy between small objects and large ones is pretty plain, and of course we don't neglect to point it out from time to time—it always comes up at the affidavit. These consequences aren't so striking, I admit; but then the general consequences of education never are particularly striking, and we are content to have a reasonably thoughtful and well-informed public for art, accounting for a major proportion of the total population. I don't think you had that, though—at least if you did I don't see why things were so generally conceded to be in such a mess."

"No," I said, " I would say that apart from a rather small group of initiates the response to serious art was divided between those who stood in awe of genius and those who rather looked down on it and thought that their five-year-old children could do as well."

"There you are, then," said the Dean. "Still, as I said before, there were signs of change even then, and change can be quite rapid once it starts. After all, speaking *sub specie aeternitatis,* it didn't take us all that long to get where we are now." With a sweep of his arm he indicated the proportions and design of the main plaza before the university, from which we had emerged.

"It just goes to show," he went on thoughtfully, "how far off futuristic speculation can be. Why, one of your people wrote a fantasy about this very year, in which he represented the whole society as a kind of police state. And of course it very easily might have been . . . ."

III

Epilogue

JON ROUSH

This review chapter states the authors' belief in the joy of learning. While the subject of our book has been the arts, the primary concern of this group of writers is the broader subject of education, and the place of the arts in that process. Our joint conclusions are that it is possible to devise a learning situation that takes into account both individual differences and the common good; that the search for order and meaning in life is the overriding objective of most students; and that the arts provide important ways to pursue this search.

Jon Roush's words sum up the book's basic message. There is no conflict between studying the arts as fields of inquiry, and learning about the arts in the context of the broader objective. It is up to the colleges to reconcile the differences that caused the apparent conflict, the differences between disciplines, between scholar and artist, and between styles. Reconciliation can come about only if colleges will make (in Jon Roush's words) "opportunity full and learning efficient" for students of all shades of talent and intellectual capability. Many faculty members and administrators would claim that this is the purpose of undergraduate education as it is now carried out. We who have written this book disagree.

The university college described in Peter Caws's "Notes on a Visit to a Distant Campus" is a typical utopia in one sense and quite atypical in another. Like most classic utopias, it envisions a social system which takes account of individual differences while promoting the common good. It assumes that a group of people, each one following his own true inclination, can be organized without inhibiting each other, so that the demands of freedom and productive order are both satisfied. Unlike other utopias, however, this one is startlingly feasible. There is nothing in this utopia which could not be implemented in a college. In fact, many of the ideas are being implemented in one institution or another already; Peter Caws's innovation is to suggest a total system built on these ideas. And not only are the techniques and technology available, but there are a significant number of people involved with education and the arts who would agree that this utopian college would be a desirable place, preferable to most colleges today. In other words, we have the means and the will to give utopia a try. The following thoughts are intended to be of some help to those who want to try.

What would it be like to build an institution where students are to be treated as free men and women? The idea that a student might define his own course of study, with some mechanism for faculty advice, would not seem very radical on many campuses which currently allow for student-initiated courses. Moreover, it is likely to become more common in the future. But what would it be like to have an entire college built on this model? Some familiar paraphernalia would disappear. There would be no catalog of courses, no major sequences, no prerequisites, perhaps no credit accounting, perhaps no grades. It is harder to say what there would be, and on that score Peter Caws's utopian vision is particularly helpful.

For the arts, two of his most interesting ideas are the concept of paradigmatic experience and the device of the affidavit. In the education of people who will not become skilled artists, one of the most difficult problems has been to find a way to provide training in the basic skills which seem necessary for any competence at all, without subjecting the student to the deadening tedium of drill. The idea of the affidavit makes a start by replacing required courses with a process of self-certification. And with advanced technology it is possible to facilitate that process. With devices for reproduction and simulation, such as cameras and tape recorders, it is possible to give "people of ordinary dexterity a paradigmatic experience of solving an aesthetic problem in some medium or other."

There will, however, undoubtedly be students for whom that solution is not sufficient, students who need the technical skills themselves. Could we really argue that a utopian, non-authoritarian system would be best for them? In the absence of an enforced structure, would students have the opportunity or patience to acquire such skills? This question is itself a paradigm of a question to be asked of any system which seeks to avoid coercion but also requires some drudgery.

It is important to ask the question in the right way. The question is not whether the opportunity for the training could be made available; the institution would simply hire people to teach the skills. Nor is the question really whether students would take advantage of the opportunity. Some would, and some would not. Certainly no one would argue that every student in a required course on technique is really taking advantage of the opportunity. There is no evidence to suggest that in a compulsory, structured system all students are either more or less likely to perform any specific tasks than they are in a non-compulsory, unstructured system. The key is the mental makeup of the student himself. Some people find the goad of outside pressure useful; others find it inhibiting. Everybody varies in this regard from time to time; and pressure or not, the person who once resisted a specific task will often later undertake it willingly as soon as he perceives a desirable outcome.

The question is: Can we devise a system which is flexible and sensitive enough to provide the right kind of motivating support for each student, together with the opportunity to acquire skills and information at the time when he is most likely to use and retain them? If such a system is possible, it cannot, as the Dean, Peter Caws's utopian guide, pointed out, be programmed in advance. If nobody can decide ahead of time what studies or activities are best for any one student, then those decisions will have to be made on the spot and frequently. Such decisions obviously require continuous sensitivity to the student's interests, capabilities, and aspirations, and there is only one person who can be relied on to have that sensitivity: the student himself. The system should of course provide him with consultants, who will be expected to have professional information of use to him. Yet although neither they nor the student should pretend that he will always make the right choices, in the final analysis the student will have more data on which to base the choices than will anyone else.

The teacher's task would be to make the opportunity full and the learning efficient. A music professor should not be expected to devise a curriculum in music which is best for all students and puts theory and technique in their proper places. But every institution should have a music professor who is able to understand what a student hopes to learn through, about, or with music and who can advise the student as to what sort of learning that objective requires and what resources are available to him at the college or elsewhere.

The consultant-teacher would not claim any final authority for knowing the best goals for his students, but it would be his responsibility to describe the best means to his students' goals. Because goals change as people work toward them, he would need to have some skill in the dialectical process of adapting his response to students' current perceptions; and he would demand a similar flexibility from students in responding to his questions and views about their education.

Merely as one example of the kind of system which could accommodate such a process, assume a freshman year that begins with a series of introductory overviews by relevant specialists. There would be live lectures, and electronically recorded or printed materials. The specialists would describe the kind of activities they normally engage in, the kind of problems they are good at, and the pertinent resources available at the college. At Peter Caws's utopian college, these overviews would be grouped according to the appropriate divisions, and they would give students at least minimal information about the strategies appropriate to different kinds of questions and an intellectual map of each division. During this period of mapping, the student would select or be assigned to a single teacher, who would serve as his chief consultant. The post of consultant would be the most prestigious in the college; it would be held by a scholar and teacher with several years' experience who would be appointed on the basis of his promise as a generalist. The consultant would help the student formulate some personal objective which could be pursued at the college—solving an historical problem, learning print-making, tutoring high school students, improving the college. The consultant would be sufficiently familiar with the faculty so that he could direct the student to other faculty members whose special expertise would be useful to the student in his studies.

Occasionally, perhaps two or three times a year, the faculty in each division would meet with the consultants to share information about students' progress. On the basis of these meetings, the faculty could make whatever plans were necessary and feasible, such as establishing *ad hoc* seminars or field trips, or arranging independent study programs. The consultants would act as liaisons between the students and the rest of the faculty and as a standing curriculum review committee.

Theoretically, the entire curriculum (if that term is still applicable) would be revised continually. In practice, the ferment would probably not be that great, because many kinds of activity would no doubt be repeated. Nevertheless, any such program would clearly present some practical difficulties. The most important difficulties are not logistical, however. The program could be administered with a student-faculty ratio of fifteen to one, giving teachers and students a lighter "course load" than is now the case. The most difficult problems would probably arise in recruiting a faculty who would be sufficiently capable of such a program and who would be willing to risk not teaching a carefully acquired specialty. The burden would be on the college to recruit and harbor such teachers, and to find ways to reassure them in the face of the conventional notions of professional behavior. In such situations there is probably nothing quite so reassuring as a high salary, although at the outset dedicated teachers would no doubt be genuinely rewarded by the excitement of participating in a revolutionary enterprise.

Utopian schemes like this are sometimes dismissed as "elitist," the argument being that they could serve only the highly motivated and intelligent student and would leave the remaining mass of students utterly nonplussed. It is true that such education requires motivation—most education does—and it is no doubt true that a number of students would not proceed very far, either because they would become interested in doing something else or because they would be incapable of coping with personal freedom. But far from serving the most intelligent only, this seems to me to be the only system flexible enough to serve students with a wide range of intellectual abilities. It would succeed as well in an open-door community college as in an elite liberal arts college.

Although it would be difficult for a totally new institution to raise sufficient money and maintain sufficient strength of nerve to establish a utopian program, a new institution is more likely to be true to such a program than would an altered existing institution. Such alterations are usually so stretched, shrunken, torn, patched and dyed by internecine quarrels that they are either deservedly discarded or tolerated as innocuous compromises. One could well argue that despite the expected rancor, the people most responsible for the institution—the governing boards, the chief officers, and the faculty—should be strong enough to implement change and to look within and without the institution for competent people to design the change. As a piece of logic, that argument is irrefutable, but as a complete guide to policy, it is utopian in the disparaging sense: it confuses what ought to be with what is. The changes we have called for would seem to me to require a thorough and fundamental restructuring of any college or university with which I am familiar. It may be that somewhere there is an institution whose leaders are selfless enough to invite and implement that kind of change and whose faculty is willing to put up with it, but it would be a rare college.

All of the preceding discussion assumes that a student should decide for himself what he will do and when he will do it. It assumes that if left to his own devices, with adequate advice from more experienced people, he will learn and practice whatever he most needs. It assumes that, in our society at least, there is nothing that must be learned by everybody in college and so nothing must be required of everybody—no essential blocks of information, no essential disciplines, and no essential skills. And finally it assumes that whatever is to be learned, there is no single best way to learn it and that in each case the procedures and sequences of learning should derive not simply from the nature of the subject matter and its traditions, nor simply from the predilections of the teacher, but primarily from the specific needs of the individual student. An institution with a faculty committed to the conventional values of their profession is not likely to accept those assumptions.

Suppose, however, that one is working within a conventional institution, encumbered with all the deadening resistance to change that a faculty normally musters. It is still possible to encourage the development in students of disciplined freedom by devising contexts for the subject matter in which questions about choice, form, self-expression, and regulation are raised. This kind of education would draw heavily on the arts and humanities.

A curriculum could be devised to investigate the question of whether there is a science of expression itself. Such a science, for example, would take full account of the commonality and difference between men who express themselves by building cities and men who construct symphonies. It would investigate the criteria for evaluating expression, for distinguishing between good and bad expression, or defining categories. A course or series of courses could be structured around different modes of expression, such as environmental or sensory modes (music, visual arts, architecture), introspective modes (myth, psychology), systematic modes (mathematics, epistemology, linguistics), and action (games, drama, ethics).

Each of these modes could presumably yield answers to aesthetic questions, and those answers should help people choose among different formulations of their own ideas and feelings, just as a scientist's concern for elegance is pertinent to his theoretical choices. Moreover, the attempt to reach such answers should refine the student's awareness of the inevitable role of the observer in establishing the form of his perceptions, just as Einstein and Heisenberg have made us aware of the role of the observer of natural phenomena.

Another example, suggested in the chapter "Education of Vision" by James Ackerman, would be a course or series of courses concerned with the study of form. An appropriate analytic structure would be threefold: natural forms, symbols and images, and man-made objects. Such a course could examine concepts like harmony, rhythm, modularity, and symmetry. In inquiring into the taxonomy of form, students would consider what necessity, if any, adheres to aesthetic standards and values and what their relation might be to the laws of nature and utility. The problems would invite the participation of all disciplines, and would benefit greatly from some kind of team teaching.

For two reasons, the kind of study represented by these two examples should probably be held up until late in a student's undergraduate career. First, such study would almost necessarily depend on materials and concepts from several conventional disciplines, and it should be assumed that the student has already been introduced to the strategies of at least one pertinent discipline (also suggested by James Ackerman) and could go on from there. That necessity would be especially pronounced if the study were centered around questions of form, structures, and expression. Students come to college impoverished in the techniques, sensitivity, and vocabulary for treating such questions.

The second and more fundamental reason for deferring such a course is that it will raise questions whose very meaning depends on the experience of the inquirer. They require maturity. To perceive fully a Picasso requires more maturity than does the understanding of calculus.

The usual argument against giving such courses to advanced students is that they are too busy preparing to be the specialists of the future to have time for a broader education. But it is exactly at the time that a man has begun to become proficient in a professional, disciplined way that he should be most ready to consider the meaning of what he is doing. Although specialization is often regarded as evil, it is so only if it closes doors, and every specialist has had the experience of having his work raise questions in apparently unrelated fields.

All of us who have shared in the writing of this book are convinced that a reformation of values is urgently in order, that the reformation must draw on artistic perception and discipline, and that such artistry cannot be regarded as the possession of professional artists alone. What has begun for us as a concern with art has necessarily led to a concern with much broader questions of education. The chief problem confronting education, as with society as a whole, is the furthering of individual freedom in the midst of imposed social organization. For the past few centuries the artist has served as the paradigm of the man who suffers the tension between his own creating voice and the mute will of his society. We believe that we have reached a time when every man must feel that tension, and live with it continually, and we believe that he will be successful to the extent that he can order his perceptions and expressions with conscious artistry. When James Ackerman talks about the necessity for self-realization, when Eric Larrabee talks about the problems of "aesthetic democracy," when Robert Watts describes his experiment in self-directed learning, each of them is describing his perception of the problems.

As we have approached the arts from this point of view in this book, we have been dealing with two fundamental and separable problems. On the one hand, we have been asking how people who are not going to be professional artists can become better educated in the arts. On the other hand, we have been asking how the arts can best be used in the education of all men. In the first case, the goals are limited to the arts specifically; but in the second, the goals are global, and the arts serve as one kind of vehicle in one kind of pedagogic strategy. If these two questions were to be used as the basis of reform, they would not lead to identical solutions. A curriculum designed to educate people in the arts would no doubt look quite different from a curriculum designed to use the arts to educate people toward some broader goal. This discrepancy explains why art faculties resist lending their talents to general education courses. Teachers of the arts argue, quite intelligently, that the understanding of art which a student achieves in a normal "interdisciplinary" course is usually so superficial as to be irrelevant to the real concerns of art and a waste of everyone's time. Their colleagues in other departments argue, equally intelligently, that a little bit is better than none at all.

Both sides, however, are attacking the problem at the wrong level. There is no theoretical conflict between the objectives of learning about art and learning about art in some larger context; on the contrary, those objectives reinforce each other in theory, and they should do so in practice as well. If the objectives do conflict within educational institutions, then there is something wrong with the institutions themselves, and it is the professional responsibility of faculties to work for appropriate institutional changes. We do not agree ourselves on everything that we would recommend, but we do agree that the situation will not be improved by having colleges simply pay more attention to the arts. If all the concerts, exhibits, lectures, and studio courses on all campuses were tripled tomorrow, we would not be much closer to utopia. We need to move the arts closer to the center of the academy and closer to the lives of the students, to find ways for people in all disciplines to become participants and makers as well as observers. To do so requires

124

that we pay attention to questions of what artistry is and how it is learned. For their part, colleges have a responsibility, as Eric Larrabee has suggested, to create new opportunities for serious interplay between their art faculties and the rest of the institution. Meanwhile, teachers of arts must broaden their idea of education in the arts so that they can devise pedagogies to bring an artistic sensibility to bear upon the entire gamut of human problems.

We are not suggesting that art become the handmaiden of some grim version of social progress. We are aware of the dangers of simplistic utilitarianism, and we believe that joy needs no excuse for being. Indeed our point is that we would welcome more joy on this planet, and if colleges are to contribute to that utopia, they must begin at home. They must make learning itself a pleasant process. The art faculties must ask themselves what they can do to help all students understand and value the joys of perception and creation, and they should begin with the premise that traditional methods have failed. Until that is done, the arts, like other endeavors pursued in universities, will suffer from a parochial version of professionalism. It is instructive, in this regard, that we have had a great deal of difficulty finding a title for this book, because although we are talking about art, we are not talking only to professional artists. Although "art" belongs in the title, we have been concerned that the word would scare away teachers and students who do not regard themselves as specialists in the fine arts. It is that attitude that has relegated art to museums and has insured that "the art of teaching" remains a hollow phrase.

Although we have concerned ourselves with undergraduate instruction in this book, any reform of higher education in line with our proposals must include the graduate schools. For the foreseeable future at least, graduate schools will be responsible for preparing the teachers of undergraduates, and it is in the graduate schools that prospective teachers will learn the conventional expectations of their profession. There they learn that a scholar's allegiance is to his profession and other scholars, not to his students, and they learn the marketing skills that will make their publications saleable but not the teaching skills to make their classes more humane. Apologists for graduate schools respond to such accusations by saying that the analysis should not be either/or, that a good teacher must also be a good scholar. Yet this defense rings hollow, because the graduate schools themselves have insisted on the "either/or" by utterly neglecting the development of teachers. Nor is the argument that good teaching cannot be taught very convincing. Although it is difficult to do, it can be done; very few schools have tried at all, and none have tried very hard. Indeed, the faculty members of graduate schools in the arts and humanities are normally ignorant of the extensive body of literature in the social and behavioral sciences concerning education. Much of that literature would help any teacher of undergraduates or graduate students, and would in the long run benefit the team work of artists and humanists.

Probably the most compelling, actual reason for graduate schools' reluctance to take seriously the task of educating teachers is that, in academic currency, there is no profit in it. Some graduate schools are famous for "producing" good scholars, but no graduate school has ever gained appreciable prestige from producing good teachers. The concern with status has similarly spelled the doom of most "intermediate degree" programs, which have attempted to train teachers but which have invariably been regarded as refuges for those who could not make it to a "real" doctorate. Nevertheless, the prestige is often much more important to department chairmen than it is to graduate students themselves, and there is absolutely no doubt that an imaginative, thorough, and intelligent program designed to prepare teachers in the arts and humanities for undergraduate colleges would attract some of the best graduate students in the country. The only thing lacking is strength of nerve on the part of the training institutions.

We insist that the arts of teaching and learning do have content and discipline. It is inescapable that no matter how intellectually advanced or specialized a man may consider himself, the need for order and meaning remains an existential fact, and the search for order and meaning necessarily leads into the domain of art. The fundamental art of our age, the art of learning, can be practiced and perfected, and its kinship to other, traditional arts is real and important. A learner practices the creative act of perceiving meaning in processes, images, and environments. As those things become less familiar, he will have to become a more artful learner.

Although we have tried in this book to offer specific suggestions for reform, we do not apologize for failing to provide a complete and flawless program. We are urging holistic changes that cannot be effected until universities change their policies in a wide number of areas, including the selection and promotion of faculty, the allocation and planning of building space, and curriculum planning. The chief request of our fellow utopians is that individual disciplines not be satisfied with tidying up their own backyards. The vitality of conventional universities and colleges is questionable, and if they do suffer a decline, it will occur for internal reasons. Healthy universities will not decay because of lack of money or because students disrupt business-as-usual. They might decay, however, because of the indifference of their faculty members to the colleges and to the students. Faculty members will not fulfill their obligation simply by furthering their discipline or by designing a more elegant curriculum. They will have to work to build institutions in which art has a chance, and they had better begin before it is too late.

APPENDIX

SUMMARY OF A 1967 SURVEY OF COLLEGE ARTS OFFERINGS

by Margaret Mahoney

In the fall of 1967 I completed a survey of existing courses and extracurricular activities at thirty-five selected colleges. The colleges were selected because as a group they offer a wide variety of programs and reveal the range of approaches in arts instruction. They do not represent a national sampling. I organized the survey under the common curriculum categories: the visual arts, theater, music, films, and interdisciplinary programs, leaving out the teaching of literature, creative writing, and dance (the first two because so much has already been written about them, and the last because too few colleges offer dance courses to allow for any generalizations). My arbitrary decision to omit these areas does not imply that I think they are unimportant in any consideration of arts offerings on a campus; quite the contrary, I believe that they must all be considered by any college in any serious review of curriculum.

The survey showed that colleges are committing themselves increasingly to greater and greater variety in the arts, hiring more faculty trained in the arts, setting up new departments to cover the arts, building large and expensive facilities, and facing increasingly large enrollments. Exactly what all the current activity adds up to is not clear. Although they all offer some kind of work in the arts, the colleges differ greatly in the seriousness with which they regard arts experience. Many students fulfill their general education requirements and are graduated without any study of or exposure to any of the arts because the colleges do not require such study or do not offer it in such a way that it would appeal to students. The discrepancy between the growth in commitment to the arts and the exclusion of arts courses from the required curriculum suggests that while colleges are giving students more opportunity for artistic experience than ever before, many have not thought through the objectives of their arts programs. In many colleges there is a curious combination of rudimentary courses and highly specialized work, which indicates a lack of fundamental philosophy of education to guide development of both curricular and extracurricular programs. The following summary of the thirty-five-college survey points up some of the discrepancies while also showing how art teaching is organized on a campus.

VISUAL ARTS

Courses in the visual arts were the first arts courses to enter the college curriculum as academic subjects and were generally labeled "the fine arts." Today they are still the dominant arts offerings on most campuses and have much heavier enrollments than other formal art areas. Depending on faculty willingness and interest, students can study painting, sculpture, drawing, design, photography, and architecture.

Traditionally, courses have been of two types: art history and studio practice. Most colleges today offer both but there are regional differences in the relative importance given the two types.

In colleges in the northeastern part of the United States, art history has tended to receive more emphasis than studio work. The first program treating art history as a serious study began a little over seventy years ago at Harvard, under Charles Eliot Norton. Similar programs were established soon after at Princeton, Yale, Columbia, and New York Universities, each of these developing strong art history programs at both the undergraduate and graduate levels. Of the five, only Yale has a studio program that is equivalent in faculty and general acceptance to the art history studies program.

In other parts of the country, studio work is usually given more prominence than art history, in facilities and in number of faculty. At many colleges, regardless of the locale, art history is taught by practicing artists on the faculty, the small colleges most often resorting to this double assignment for the artist because of their difficulty in obtaining art historians from the currently insufficient supply.

In general, the universities offering courses concerned with the visual arts have at least two departments. Where art history was well entrenched in the curriculum before studio work was introduced, as on the East Coast, the art department does not consider studio work an academic subject and therefore wants it in a separate, distinct category. In the universities where studio came in first or has always held a dominant position, the result is also two separate departments with studio receiving much larger financial support from the university. The combination of history and studio in one department is rare. The best-known examples are Stanford, Indiana and Georgia.

All of the thirty-five colleges in my survey, and I suspect that this is true for most colleges, now offer introductory courses in the history of art as credit toward the general education requirement. While some treat the arts differently within an interdisciplinary course, none appear to have completely abandoned the traditional art history surveys. According to the 1966 College Art Association survey, the colleges favor the chronological historical survey course over the non-historical introductory course by a ratio of twenty to one.

The studio program at a typical college is a series of progressively more difficult courses, most of which are open to any students who have taken the beginning course. A few schools offer studio courses designed specifically for non-majors who want a chance to work with art materials. The crafts, rather than painting and sculpture, are offered sometimes in such courses. At the time of my survey, Grinnell sponsored non-credit workshops in the crafts while Indiana and Georgia offered the non-arts major courses for credit in crafts. Smith had a course in materials and techniques open only to students who were planning to take other art courses, and Mount Holyoke had two one-credit courses in drawing and watercolor open to all students.

What I have described here is the traditional approach to visual arts courses. Some colleges offer other approaches that take into account a student's unfamiliarity with or lack of interest in visual art forms. Courses in visual design at Massachusetts Institute of Technology (MIT), offered by the department of architecture in the school of architecture and planning, involve the students in problems of visual invention, organization, and expression, to encourage visual awareness. The department also offers similar courses in photography. At Kalamazoo College there are introductory courses designed to develop appreciation and understanding of architecture, sculpture, and painting through study of what and how the artist sees, as well as a study of his tools and materials. Students who want studio work, whether they are majors or non-majors, must first take a special course in the practice of art in which they explore problems in creative work and learn to use various media.

There is no strong tradition for student-generated or student-operated activity in the visual as in other arts areas. But now there are signs that students are becoming more actively interested. Emory University has a new reciprocal relation with the Atlanta School of Art as the result of a mass appearance of Emory students before their president to ask for some opportunity to work creatively. Students at Stanford decided to exhibit their own work, deliberately choosing not to have the department of art's sponsorship. The general and increasing interest in photography and film-making has also resulted in more student exhibitions and in a desire of students to have their own work space and access to college-owned facilities in off hours.

THEATER

Theater study is not an established academic area. Not until the 1950's did colleges begin to hire faculty and introduce work for credit. Today, however, few new colleges open their doors without a theater department while few existing colleges are without at least some course work. Enrollment in theater courses tends to be low in proportion to total enrollment in the colleges, but there is a somewhat higher percentage of students involved in play productions.

All of the colleges in my survey offered courses on plays as literature. Many also offered courses in theater techniques, the art of acting, of producing and directing plays, and sometimes of playwriting. In addition these colleges all have facilities for performance—as do most liberal arts colleges in this country.

The least comprehensive programs in theater, offered by one-third of the thirty-five colleges surveyed, consist of literary courses in drama, usually sponsored by the department of English. Two or three of these English departments require the beginning student to consider problems of production or do practical production work in addition to reading.

The other colleges have a department of theater or dramatic art, or a department of speech and drama. The former usually emphasize the historical survey, although some colleges offer theater criticism (New York University and Stanford are examples), and Wesleyan offers "Frontiers of the Theater," a course open to all students, in which the theme is man's confrontation with the world in ritual, propaganda, play, and psychodrama. The departments of speech and drama, usually found in small, independent colleges, stress the practical side of theater—the techniques of acting, directing, and producing. Some institutions offer drama courses within both the theater and literature departments.

Fewer than half of the colleges included in the survey offer theater courses as one of several options that fulfill the general education requirement. (Other options are usually music, visual arts, and literature. Literature courses often cover some drama, but do not include it as a central area of study.) Nine of the thirty-five colleges provide introductory courses on theater as electives only.

The colleges also differ greatly in the amount of theater study open to or provided expressly for non-majors. The usual introductory course in theater is an appreciation course. At New York University, courses in drama open to non-majors emphasize diction and experiments in contemporary theater. At Wesleyan, the course mentioned earlier and another one providing production experience are open to all students.

The school of creative arts at Brandeis offers a number of courses for the non-major. "Introduction to Drama and the Theater," a survey of dramatic literature and theory and "The Actor's Art," an introduction to the nature of both acting and directing, are open to all students. In the latter course the emphasis is not on training talent, but students are provided stage experience through the use of workshop sessions, films, recordings, and the study of acting and directing methods, both past and present.

Courses in Yale's school of drama are open to junior and senior non-majors, but the school does not encourage "non-serious" students to take them. Historical courses in drama for the general student at Yale are offered by the department of English.

There is no prototype of the theater or drama instructor; some are professors with degrees from schools of education, others have doctorates in literature and other fields, and still others lack advanced degrees but have had years of specialized training in the theater.

On a few campuses a professional theatrical group is in residence for all or part of the year. Arrangements between the colleges and universities and these groups differ widely, but in some cases professional actors and directors are teaching as well as giving performances.

Running parallel to any formal course work in the colleges is the theater-workshop or playhouse, started and often maintained by students. The drama group can even flourish within institutions—such as Johns Hopkins—that lack a theater department or anyone on the faculty directly connected with the theater. On many campuses the theater group is the oldest art activity. Some groups go back to the nineteenth century; an example is Princeton's Triangle Club, founded in 1893, which produces musical shows written and performed by students.

At the time of my survey, only a few colleges—Antioch, the University of California at Berkeley, and Stanford are examples—offered credit, variable though it is, for theater (as well as musical) performance.

MUSIC

I have found no information to indicate precisely when music became a recognized academic area but it seems fairly certain that until at least the mid-1930's it was not considered a necessary part of the college curriculum. Just at that point in history Carnegie Corporation, on the advice of a group from the worlds of music and education, decided to provide colleges with specially selected sets of musical recordings and phonographic equipment. This was intended not only to help fill the leisure hours of students but also to stimulate requests for formal study in music.

Today in college curricula the great majority of music offerings are courses *about* music—that is, they are concerned with appreciation, history, theory, and (rarely) composition. Most colleges also offer students some opportunity for training in performance—in singing or playing an instrument, and most provide some opportunity to perform in bands, orchestras, choral groups, or small ensembles.

In my survey I included Howard, Michigan, Indiana, and Oberlin, which have schools of music and have large and excellent faculties that offer courses in theory and history, as well as applied music, to those students in the college not working toward a music school degree. Twenty-eight of the thirty-five colleges in the review have departments of music. They vary in caliber and capacity. Some combine theory, appreciation, and history with instruction in performance; others limit courses to the non-performance areas only. Many of the departments are staffed with professionally able people who have been trained at schools of music. Some of the small, independent colleges, on the other hand, have meager staffs not capable of providing advanced work, and do not offer a wide choice of courses.

Two institutions—MIT and Franklin and Marshall—have no separate departments of music and no music major, but do offer courses in music. Johns Hopkins was the only institution in the survey that offered no courses in music or pertaining to music.

Seven of the thirty-five colleges made no distinction between the major and the non-major in their music offerings; the non-major takes the same theory or introductory literature courses as the major. Other colleges such as Princeton, Yale, and Brandeis made no distinction in selected history courses. At Grinnell an introductory course is the prerequisite for most music courses for both majors and non-majors, but two literature courses ("Music in America" and "Contemporary Music") are open to all as electives.

MIT's introductory courses expose students to the literature of music and to the art of listening; second-level courses building on these deal with theory in its historical perspective; and there are seminars for thorough study of specific works.

Two-thirds of the colleges in the survey have at least one course especially for the non-major, with the emphasis on theory and materials. Five offered a course covering literature and history. Skidmore's introduction to music for non-majors covers elements of music, instruments of the orchestra, and representative works of selected composers. Pomona has two music courses for non-majors, and Georgia has a listener's history course and a special music course for visual arts majors. Stanford and Michigan have special courses emphasizing forms (for example, opera or symphony), and Wellesley has two one-credit courses in historical periods. Harvard's introductory course gives the non-major training in listening through a combination of theory, materials, and history.

Somewhat specialized approaches to teaching the non-major are going on at Indiana, where the school of music believes that courses for these students should be taught not by the professional musician but by someone who knows that he must "sell" music to the students. The result is an introductory course which covers the evolution of music in a cultural milieu, a representative sample of compositions, and a technique for listening. Other electives are in appreciation and history. Any student may take the school's freshman theory course two days a week; the other three days are intensive drill sessions for ear training, open to majors only.

At Michigan, Earl Moore (now chairman of the music department at the University of Houston) began a pattern of instruction that greatly increased enrollment in introductory music. For the non-major he offered practical training in the art of listening, and the history of music taught by an instructor who is neither a professional musician nor a highly specialized musicologist, but a violinist with a Ph.D. in English literature. Each semester there is a waiting list for this course, which at the time of my survey required three sections to meet the demand. The non-major at Michigan can also take more advanced courses. Moore introduced the same approach at Houston, and enrollment in the introductory course reportedly shot up each semester.

Non-majors at Antioch can study harmony and counterpoint, but the student must read music to qualify for enrollment. In fact, Antioch's catalog suggests that anyone planning to attend the college should have some musical training. This is the only college in the survey that makes training in one of the arts a possible criterion for admission .

Wesleyan University's courses in tribal, folk, and popular music, which are offered to all students, was the only specially designed series relating to the contemporary scene that I found in my survey.

The opportunities for instruction in voice or an instrument vary but are usually obtainable. At an independent college, like Bryn Mawr, which does not maintain a faculty of professional musicians, students are charged extra for instruction and may have to travel to get it. And at some of the best-known eastern colleges the student can study through special arrangements with a local music school. The catalogs do not state that an off-campus arrangement has to be made but specify only that instruction is provided when a student requests it.

The chances at most colleges to perform are numerous. Indiana offers performance opportunities in ensembles for wind, brass, and stringed instruments, and a jazz group, in addition to bands, the orchestra, and a special freshman mixed chorus for non-music majors. Students receive one hour of credit for work with a performing group. Indiana also allows limited credit for instruction.

Students at the University of Georgia must make a two-year commitment to the band, orchestra, or chorus but anyone is eligible, and participants receive credit. Wesleyan pays students who join the choir.

Many of the campus groups are of excellent quality—the Harvard Glee Club, for example, has one of the most sophisticated repertories in the country.

Since the early 1950's there has been a trend for ensembles of professional musicians to become residents of a college where they perform and sometimes teach. At colleges with no music department or no practicing musicians on the faculty, a resident quartet may be the only source of musical experience, and its presence on campus can be influential in getting more music into the curriculum in the future.

FILM

Like courses in the other arts, courses in film fall into two categories: those that stress study *about* the art and those that stress practicing it. Some deal with the history of film or attempt to foster appreciation of the art form or of films as a means of communication; others concern the techniques of film-making.

The dichotomy between majors and non-majors, however, is not so marked in film work as it is in the other arts; the majority of the students in film courses seem to be non-majors. And the problem of motivating students to take courses should not apply here, since the appearance of film courses is largely due to the pressure of students whose interest in films is demonstrated by the countless student-formed societies on campuses across the country.

Film courses are the most recent addition to the college arts curriculum, and they have proliferated rapidly since the 1950's. Of the 35 colleges I reviewed, 13 offer courses in films. Yet another survey shows that in 1964-1965 the 100 largest colleges in the United States were giving a total of 846 courses on film (this figure includes both undergraduate and graduate offerings). Over 50 of these 100 institutions appear to offer instruction in film-making or the opportunity to produce films. The largest creative production centers are usually big institutions: the University of California at Los Angeles (UCLA), the University of Southern California, Columbia, New York University, North Carolina, Miami, and Baylor. Each offers 10 or more courses in film-making. One notable exception to this rule is Antioch College. Work in film is not formalized within any department at Antioch, but creative film-making has a definite place on campus.

Still another survey gives some information on the faculty who teach film courses. Until recently, these courses have been taught mostly by film-makers or critics—people close to the creative side of the subject. Now, however, professors of philosophy, drama, art, history, literature, and music are taking on an increasing percentage of the non-technical courses on film. One program, widely recognized as useful, is directed by a graduate of a teachers' college whose interest is in the psychology of film. The film-makers and critics sometimes question whether these "film-buffs" know enough to make competent teachers.

Film courses are offered by a wide variety of departments in colleges and universities: departments or schools of education, speech and drama, radio and television, journalism, or fine arts.

As courses on films become more widespread—and they are literally springing up overnight—the problems inherent in designing them are proving to be similar to those in the visual arts. Many critics of the present offerings feel that the predominant survey-appreciation courses are not meeting the general student's real needs and that perhaps what is required is something that lies between the historical survey and courses in techniques—a program that can teach the general student to think in terms of film as a creative mode of expression and get to know some of its possibilities and limitations. Other criticism is that courses in film-making are training film directors, who, like the painters and sculptors produced by college studio programs, are finding that the real world offers few opportunities to practice the art they have studied.

An example of the kind of historical survey typical of most college film programs is the sequence of two courses on motion pictures and television offered at Skidmore. These constitute a chronological review, beginning with early silent films. As on other campuses, the entire college community can attend the films shown for these courses.

This chronological approach has been criticized by those teaching and creatively involved in making films. In the words of a film-maker teaching at UCLA: ". . . there is an irrational quality to art which irritates and confounds those who are trying to put knowledge of art into systems. That is why art studies sometimes seem out of place in the academy, and why so much pressure is put upon teachers of film by colleagues in other departments to adopt their methodology. In many other disciplines, especially in the humanities, scholars seek causal lines to explain everything, for without the patterns which emerge with this approach they fear they have no subject, there is no intellectual content, and they do not belong in an academy."

Some colleges and universities are, however, departing from the two main patterns. At Harvard, the series of courses for non-arts majors in visual composition (mentioned earlier under visual arts) leads logically into an array of unusual courses in light and photography. These begin with still photography and progress to animation and motion pictures.

The Communications Arts Group at New York University offers courses on film as part of a program that provides work in dramatic art, journalism, television, cinema, and radio. Any student at the college can take these courses; there is no major. The courses on film cover both relevant techniques—producing, directing, writing—and the art and history of cinema.

INTERDISCIPLINARY PROGRAMS

For a number of years both Columbia University and the University of Chicago have required all students to take a sequence in the humanities extending through nine quarters. The objectives have been to acquaint each student with the major achievements in literature, music, and the visual arts, build his skill in interpreting artistic works, give him an understanding of the principles upon which critical judgments and evaluations in the arts are made, and develop his ability to write about these principles. Chicago has brought in as lecturers practicing artists and others directly involved in the creative process to enhance its program, to relieve the regular faculty (who may be essentially not interested in interdisciplinary teaching since it tears them away from their specialties), and to inject some excitement into the courses.

Berea College's one-year required humanities course integrates literature, the visual arts, and music; all art departments cooperate in it, with each faculty presenting its own offering. The course is organized around several functional units—creative man, social man, contemplative man, worshipping man—an approach entirely different from that of the standard survey. Berea offers a selection of works from various art media to illustrate the artists' concern with the particular theme being discussed. Studio experience is an important part of the program, and is run as a laboratory course.

Until five or six years ago Kenyon College had no required courses in the arts; according to the dean of the college, "Most of the Kenyon graduates, it could fairly be said, left us as ignorant of the arts as they were when they entered the college." Kenyon has now introduced a new freshman-sophomore general education requirement of which the arts are an integral part. The new curriculum gives each student direct exposure to what the dean calls "the major shaping forces of our culture," providing basic courses in each of five areas—natural sciences, philosophy, history, the arts, and literature. By the end of their sophomore year students have completed a course that considers the common features in music, drama, and the visual arts and their special distinctions.

At Scripps College all students must take a sequence of courses called "Humanities," which form the core of the curriculum in general education. "Cultural self-understanding" for the student is the aim of this sequence, which seems to be a chronological survey covering the major ideas and personalities of our civilization. This traditional approach is enriched in content by its heavy reliance on examples from the arts.

A new program for all freshmen was introduced a year ago as an experiment at Antioch. It features individualized instruction to suit a student's needs and interests with special core studies which are broad, integrated approaches to the physical sciences, the social sciences, and the humanities. The latter covers history, foreign languages, design, theater, literature, music, philosophy, and religion. Interdisciplinary lectures on a theme are balanced by seminars, independent study, workshops in the arts, and extracurricular activities—all supposedly integrated to make a whole. The art workshops are for students to learn the techniques of graphics, dramatic arts, and music.

A special degree-granting interdepartmental program at Earlham College offers study and practice in graphic arts, music, and drama to students who want a general background in the fine arts. A seminar in the arts, also operated on an interdepartmental basis, is open to non-majoring upperclassmen who have the instructors' consent to enroll. It offers a chance to discuss and criticize works in art, music, and theater. Recently Earlham introduced an experimental, introductory course for underclassmen, also open to non-majors, under the label "M.A.D." (music, art, drama). The student in this course enrolls in one area, but also hears lectures and does assignments in the other areas.

At Mount Holyoke any senior can enroll in an interdepartmental course entitled "Art and Reality." The emphasis is on applying aesthetic theory to the visual arts; specific works of philosophy, literature, painting, sculpture, and architecture are used to illustrate the theory of art as mimesis and the theory of symbolic form.

Harvard offers considerable interdisciplinary work in the visual arts. The committee on the practice of the visual arts sponsors a series of such courses, and others are offered by departments such as fine arts and architecture.

Wesleyan requires all freshmen to take a one-semester, no-credit workshop in the humanities which gives students an opportunity to participate in various forms of artistic experience. The workshop's director is the head of the art department.

THE ARTISTIC ENVIRONMENT

The multi-purpose auditorium or theater and the small exhibition hall or gallery on campus are disappearing as more and more colleges and universities construct centers of performing arts and design impressive museum buildings. As a rule the large universities construct the large performing arts centers, but the smaller independent colleges are also putting up some interesting facilities.

Dartmouth, for example, has a multi-million-dollar complex which now operates all year, serving the Hanover and nearby New Hampshire community as much as the college itself. This center provides the latest in equipment for film showing, stage production, concerts, and exhibits of experimental art.

Rhode Island University has opened the first four buildings of a fine arts center that is eventually to contain twelve buildings; it will have an experimental theater as well as a regular one, a 600-seat recital hall, studios for art work, and practice rooms. Syracuse is breaking ground for a center in a year and a half; meanwhile, a special committee is studying the artistic resources and potentials of the region. The Annenberg School of Communications at the University of Pennsylvania is finishing a new performing arts center whose distinctive feature is said to be "the wedding of communications research with performing arts." The center will feature drama and music and will house theaters, rehearsal halls, practice rooms, and research facilities. The equipment in some of these newer campus theaters cannot be matched on most professional stages. Carnegie-Mellon University will be designing a new theater building that will also house the design department, and will be next door to Pittsburgh's educational television station's new facility, a deliberate interlocking so that theater, design, and television can be encouraged to collaborate.

A far older idea than that of having a performing arts center on a campus, is having an art museum located at a college or university. The first five college art museums were set up in the nineteenth century at Yale, Stanford, Bowdoin, Princeton, and Harvard. By 1930 eight more had appeared, at Mount Holyoke, Michigan, Mills, Oberlin, Minnesota, Smith, Vassar, and Williams. As of 1951 only three other institutions—MIT, the University of California at Berkeley, and Amherst —had joined the list. The early 1950's saw a boom in campus art museum construction; fourteen new museums appeared in 1952-1966, and other institutions renovated or expanded existing facilities.

Of the thirty-five colleges I reviewed, twenty-seven have art museums. Nine of these were built in the late nineteenth or early twentieth centuries, eleven between 1946 and 1960, and seven between 1960 and 1966. Within the next year or so Wisconsin, Iowa, California at Berkeley, Kansas, Minnesota, and Williams will complete new facilities.

The artist-in-residence programs already mentioned in connection with teaching mean that, for those campuses which house professional actors or musicians, there is a good source of performing talent on hand. In addition, institutions with professional schools of music or drama can provide their own local concert series. The school of music at Indiana, for example, gives over five hundred concerts, excluding opera productions, in one year, all free to students. These events are also well attended by people living in the surrounding community. At Kalamazoo the faculty, students, and resident artists of the music department present many concerts and productions. The college also sponsors a yearly Bach festival, using a special chorus and orchestra made up of residents of the community as well as people on campus.

Colleges and universities—even the smallest—invite outside performers throughout the year. Some institutions have concert and museum managers who have year-round programs of shows and exhibits. Their revolving budgets for bookings run from $50,000 for many small colleges to $500,000 for large institutions. Small colleges often group regionally to attract performers and shows to their area. In addition to regular artist-booking agencies, there are also a few small but active non-profit organizations concerned exclusively with booking performing artists at colleges and universities.

In sponsoring musical and theatrical events on campus the colleges and universities can be in keen competition with commercially arranged programs in nearby towns. But in providing one kind of artistic event—film showings—these institutions can sometimes offer programs unobtainable off campus.

As of 1966, there were nearly four thousand film societies in the United States; many campuses had more than one. This is an enormous increase over the two hundred reported in 1952. Most film societies are student-run; the presence of more than one group usually indicates that some students were dissatisfied with what the first was showing. Often the student union sponsors a series containing mostly entertainment films, while the film society or societies sponsor so-called art films.

This interest of students in seeing films matches in intensity the growing student interest in making films. These two developments are by far the most explicit statement we have of growing student concern about the arts, but many students would be unlikely to label an interest in film as an artistic concern. They would be more likely to say that it is an interest in communications, and in their own minds fail to see the interconnection. The fault in their reasoning is of course the fault of an education that has failed to show them that the arts and communications are indeed interconnected.

COLLEGES IN THE SURVEY

Amherst College, Amherst, Massachusetts
Antioch College, Yellow Springs, Ohio
Berea College, Berea, Kentucky
Brandeis University, Waltham, Massachusetts
Bryn Mawr College, Bryn Mawr, Pennsylvania
University of California, Berkeley, California
University of Chicago, Chicago, Illinois
Colby College, Waterville, Maine
Earlham College, Richmond, Indiana
Franklin and Marshall College, Lancaster, Pennsylvania
University of Georgia, Athens, Georgia

Grinnell College, Grinnell, Iowa
Harvard University, Cambridge, Massachusetts
Howard University, Washington, D.C.
Indiana University, Bloomington, Indiana
Johns Hopkins University, Baltimore, Maryland
Kalamazoo College, Kalamazoo, Michigan
*Kenyon College, Gambier, Ohio
Massachusetts Institute of Technology, Cambridge, Massachusetts
University of Michigan, Ann Arbor, Michigan
Mount Holyoke College, South Hadley, Massachusetts
New York University, New York, New York
Oberlin College, Oberlin, Ohio
Pomona College, Claremont, California
Princeton University, Princeton, New Jersey
Scripps College, Claremont, California
Skidmore College, Saratoga Springs, New York
Smith College, Northampton, Massachusetts
Stanford University, Stanford, California
Swarthmore College, Swarthmore, Pennsylvania
Trinity College, Washington, D.C.
Wellesley College, Wellesley, Massachusetts
Wesleyan University, Middletown, Connecticut
Western College for Women, Oxford, Ohio
Wilson College, Chambersburg, Pennsylvania
Yale University, New Haven, Connecticut

---

* Kenyon was not in the survey of thirty-five colleges, except for its
interdisciplinary work.

A SHORT SELECTED BIBLIOGRAPHY
FOR READING AND REFERENCE

Arts in Society. "Symposium: The Role of the University as a Cultural Leader in Society." University of Wisconsin Extension Division, Vol. 3, No. 4, Summer 1966.

Astin, Alexander W. *et al.* "National Norms for Entering College

Freshmen." Fall 1966, 1967, 1968, *ACE Research Reports* (American Council on Education, Washington, D.C.).

Bell, Daniel. *The Reforming of General Education.* New York: Columbia University Press, 1966.

Brown, John Nicholas (Chm.). *Report on the Committee on the Visual Arts at Harvard University.* Cambridge: Harvard University, 1956.

Bruner, Jerome S. *Toward a Theory of Instruction.* Cambridge: The Belknap Press of Harvard University, 1966.

Burnham, Jack. "Systems Esthetics," Artforum, Vol. VII, No. 1, September 1968, pp. 31-35.

Copland, Aaron. *What to Listen for in Music.* New York: Mentor Books, 1964.

Coulson, William R., and Carl Rogers, eds. *Man and the Science of Man.* Columbus: Charles E. Merrill, 1968.

Craik, Kenneth H. "The Prospects for an Environmental Psychology." University of California, Berkeley: Institute of Personality Assessment and Research. Research Bulletin, 1966. Mimeographed.

Dance: A Projection for the Future. The Developmental Conference on Dance, paperbound. University of California, Los Angeles. San Francisco: Impulse Publications, 1968.

Dennis, Lawrence E. and Renate M. Jacob, eds. *The Arts in Higher Education.* Jossey-Bass Inc., 1968.

Dennis, Lawrence E. and Joseph F. Kauffman, eds. *College and the Student.* American Council on Education, 1966.

Directory of American College Theatre. Washington, D.C.: American Educational Theatre Association, Inc. First Edition 1960, paperbound. Second edition, 1967, paperbound.

The Fine Arts and the University. The Frank Gustein Lectures, 1965. A. Whitney Griswold, John P. Coolidge, F. Curtis Canfield, Vincent J. Scully, Edward F. Sekler. Toronto: The Macmillan Company of Canada Ltd. in association with York University, 1965.

"The Future of the Humanities." *Daedalus,* Vol. 98, No. 3. Summer 1969. Cambridge: American Academy of Arts and Sciences.